Sex: Everything You Didn't Know You Needed to Know

M. Christian & Ralph Greco Jr.

Introduction by Amy Marsh

C O N N E C T with the publisher:

Substack:	parisianphoenixpublishing.substack.com
Web:	www.ParisianPhoenix.com
Facebook	@parisianphoenixpublishing
Instagram:	@ parisianphoenix
LinkedIn	@parisianphoenixpublishing
Patreon	@parisianphoenix
TikTok	@parisianphoenix
X:	@parisbirdbooks

PARISIAN PHOENIX
PUBLISHING

CONTENTS

ACKNOWLEDGMENTS

"If sex is such a natural phenomenon, how come there are
so many books on how to do it?"
—BETTE MIDLER

While many great people helped make this (we hope) fun book, there are (alas) too many to list here. But we wouldn't be able to sleep at night without tipping our *chapeaux* to the folx who were the best of the best of the best: *thank you, everyone!*

Amy Marsh, who wrote an amazing, and oh-so-flattering introduction.

Jean Marie Stine, who first got us started here (and there and there) and then to Angel Ackerman who took up the mantle, or ran with the ball or…Hell, she got us here, a million thanks (or is it spanks?) Angel! The fantastic people we interviewed — you made this book shine, Dawn Mostow and Ms. Ava.

The experts who corrected our mistakes, though any errors (and we know there'll be more than a few) are purely our fault, so blame us and not them.

And finally, everyone out there who reads our little missive and cracks a smile, chuckles even just the smallest amount, and, best of all, is inspired to learn about the ins-and-outs, and ins-and-outs and ins-and-outs of safe, responsible, conscientious, consensual, and enjoyable *sex!*

A NOTE FROM THE AUTHORS

"I believe that sex is one of the most beautiful, natural,
wholesome things that money can buy."
—STEVE MARTIN

Congratulations, you're about to learn everything you have ever wanted to know about sex from two of the handsomest [*you flatterer*], sexually knowledgeable, attractive [*and then some*], straight-but-not narrow [*I prefer kinkier-than-hell*] fellows ever to put pen to paper.

But before we get into it, let's get serious for a moment, though I am serious about some of the above [*serious=last refuge of the humorless*]. Chris [*M.Christian to most folx*] and I decided that it was about time to give forth on some combined non-fiction sex scribblings [*not that anybody was asking for them, but still…*], and even interview a few experts [*blackmail is our friend*] to put this, our first, co-authored-though-not-to-be-our-last [*you delightful optimist*] tome out into the world.

We even manage to interview each other at the end of this all, which is probably the silliest part of the book [*and that's saying something*], seeing how well we know one another. But it all did come out wonderfully I feel [*no disagreement here*] — and here you have it.

This all started as Chris and I sat in the airport about to leave St. Louis [*a fantastic time*], having come from yet another successful run at the "Beat Me In St. Louis" kink lifestyle weekend [*don't forget the kick-ass BBQ*] where we taught three classes. As always, it was a grand ole' hang with my bestest buddy [*right back at ya*], and as we sat there jawing over the writing biz, as Chris and I often do when in each other's company, this book idea was born.

And we managed it all while beating back the autograph seekers and paparazzi.

Why not pen something fun [*always*], informative [*as much as possible*] and encompassing the full range, or at least as much of the home-on-the-range we could imagine of sex? Why not groove on those great feelings we get at our classes? Why not use our rapier-like wit, or dull-edged Wilkinson blade, [*and only a few fart jokes*] to poke some holes in assumptions [*lots of 'ass' in assumptions*], expose a little of our doubts and fears [*whimper/whine*] and have a grand old time talking about that subject we talk and write about most of the time anyway [*only thing better than writing about sex is having sex, and then writing about it*].

As is true of our classes, and generally how Chris and I are as people, as opposed to how we are as beavers [*my spirit animal*], we've tried to keep things light in what follows, interjecting as much humor as possible [*okay, maybe three fart jokes ... tops*]. Yes, you'll still get lots of insert-tab-A-into-slot-B instructions in what follows. Chris is truly an expert of many arts and has a deep knowledge and a clear way of explaining the intricacies of various practices [*my tabs and various slots being frequently used*]. Still, hopefully, we're also going to get some chuckles from you as well [*please laugh ... please, please laugh*].

Also along the way, you'll also come across some activities/play/practices of which we are not so enamored. We aren't saying that you shouldn't have at that voodoo that you do. Please do what you will, to your heart's content, or for however long an orifice will stretch [*lube ... lots and lots and lots of lube ... voice of experience here*], but the codicil we often hear ourselves saying in a class after we expound on an activity we aren't fans of is: *"Well, unless, of course, you're into that sort of thing."* Really, whatever your thing is, fine. We aren't judging [*never ... okay, now and again to be honest about it and then we hate ourselves for that all-too human of frailties*]. There are just some things that aren't our thing, and we felt we were duty-bound to tell you what we are and are not into, give the reason we aren't into them [*mostly for safety's sake*] but to expound on these activities all the same, with as much honesty and humor as we did the rest of the stuff here.

You do want us to be honest, right?

You'll see that this book is divided into two sections, the regular sex stuff [*wheee!*] and what people call *kinky* [*extra WHEEEE!*]. It's hard to define what is precisely kinky for each person, akin to 'You say potato, I say smother me in chives' [*with the whole chicken*]. But what Chris and I have included in the kink section, we feel, falls into the broad category of what people may come to consider 'non-vanilla' (see our glossary for a definition of that term) sexual activity [*until you try it, of course*].

Some of this stuff might be your everyday go-to, the 'default browser' in your intimate world; other things might be those sextivities you have thought about and are looking to try very soon. Still, others might be nothing you'd touch with a ten-foot pole [*just remember the lube ... always lube*].

Also, please take note that while Chris and I are mostly heterosexual-leaning people [*though always willing to lean to an experiment or two*], we've nevertheless strived to make this book as gloriously inclusive as possible. So, if you feel our wacky wordplay has excluded or insulted you in *any* way, we're sincerely sorry. Sex is something that everyone, if they wish to, should enjoy [*do I need to mention lube again?*] no matter who you want to do it with/for/or at/over or under. Our intention is always to include everybody, but sometimes we err...we are only naked apes after all.

And as is also true with our classes, our lives in general, I'd like to think that Chris and I are ever learning and humble enough to realize that we don't know it all and welcome questions and comments [*and nude pics*]. If you have ever seen us live [*luckily, so far, no one has yet to see us dead*] you will notice that we don't as much take a classic 'time out' for Q and A's—we just have people raise their hands [*or other body parts where applicable*] whenever they want to throw out something [*please, no canned goods*]. While we won't see it if you raise your hand when reading this book, we do invite you to shoot us over any questions, comments, or advice, [*and nudes*] you might have.

Contact us also for how to donate to the M.Christian/Ralph Greco Jr. fund for the *Perpetually Immature Yet Exceedingly Handsome* [*our board meetings are a blast*], a [*sadly*] non-profit organization helping to better the lives of two writers you will get to know quite well the more you read [*and maybe we'll send you nudes as well*].

We thank you very much [*and then some!*] plunking down your cash to buy this book and investing your precious time to give it a read. May you continue to have peace, happiness, good health, and great sex in your life [*and the lives of all those you love*], and if you don't yet have any or all of these things, we do wish you them, in spades, forever here on.

Ralph, from the wilds of suburban New Jersey
[Chris, from the People's Republic of Eugene, Oregon]

SECTION I: THE EVERYDAY STUFF

INTRODUCTION

Individually and in tandem, Ralph Greco and M.Christian have considerable expertise and experience as sex writers, sex educators, and sexual *bon vivants*. Here they've penned a breezy, jaunty book about sex that provides a great introduction to "the basics" as well as many of the more exotic, erotic pleasures to be had with one or more adult human bodies.

As a clinical sexologist and certified sexuality educator, I appreciate many things about this book, including the authors' emphasis on safety and consent and their efforts to remove binary gender references from most of the content, unless they are specifically necessary. I also appreciate the amount of time spent dealing with several forms of kink and BDSM.

I also enjoyed the inclusion of respectful and insightful interviews with Miss Ava (ex-proprietor of The Sissy Parlor), and Dawn Mostow (Dawnamatrix Designs). If I have any criticism of the book, it's that I found myself wanting a few more of these additional voices.

In spite of the range of topics covered, this book won't be everyone's first choice for comprehensive coverage of human sexuality. For one thing, the book is written with quite a lot of humor, asides, puns, and a generally ribald, romping tone. If the Car Talk guys, Click and Clack, had written a book about sex, it might have turned out a bit like Ralph G. and M.Christian's tome. In other words, many of the jokes land as "guy humor" and for some readers, this may not be what they want. But other readers will find the humor enjoyable and will also respond to the impulses of kindness and hope that inform this book. These readers will understand that the authors really do wish them to have fun while they frolic, and so they made their messages supportive and their knowledge accessible to those who need it the most, in a way that is hip and entertaining.

I've got hundreds of books about human sexuality, with room on my shelves for more. I'd place this one next to Paul Joannide's *Guide to Getting It On* and Michael Castleman's *Sizzling Sex for Life*.

Ralph and M.Christian, you done good.

Amy Marsh, Ed.D, DHS
Springfield, Ore.
2025

CHAPTER 1:
First Things First

Let's talk about consent.

Do we have your consent to talk about it? This is a big one, kids!

The 'C' word, **consent**, is crucial stuff. And the world has been waking up to the concept. But not because it's politically correct, but because it's the right thing, the way two (or more) people should approach one another. The very best way to play fairly with those around you, no matter what it is you might be playing at.

Look, we hear and see the blow-back over this issue as much as you. The worried overreactions about insisting that sexual consent be clearly requested, clearly communicated, clearly received, and clearly given — *omg* (again). Maybe you worry all that caution is going to take the spontaneity out of sex, or that soon will come the criminalization of flirting, or that 'they' are going to take the fun out of *everything*.

Surely, we should rail against secret sex police clapping any of us in irons (and not the good and kinky ones we'll talk about later in this book) and hauling the good citizens of Gotham to the Rainbow Gulag. But consent isn't about putting speed bumps in the bedroom, or anywhere else for that matter.

Consent focuses on treating other people with empathy.

Hey, you don't like it when somebody does things to you without permission, right? That's all we are talking about here. Keep your hands, or anything else, off my rhubarb unless you know it's okay to fondle my rhubarb,

So, how do you do this consent thing? Well, peachy. (Please tell us if it's not okay for us to call you peachy, okay?) You have a lot of challenging work to do ...

Kidding!!!

All you do is fucking *ask!*

Do you mind me flirting? Do you mind me touching you? Do you want to have sex? What kind of sex would you be comfortable with? Do you want me to send you a blurry picture of my junk? Might I see/salivate over/put a picture of yours into a discreetly marked file on my computer?

Inherent in our actions and speech should be the above questions, if not outright uttered, when you come to that juncture when things are not so clearly delineated, and even sometimes when they are. Those moments when you feel a twinge of "don't cross over into that lane, bucko" that we all get as the caring and feeling species we call human, that's when the sudden question of "Ya know, I wonder if?" should pop into our brains. Or maybe we get that sinking gut lurch of "Hey, that person seems to not like me standing here so much" when you need to take a step back, sometimes literally, to reassess what you thought was a witty and stylish come-on. You know, when the person you have approached is actually saying "Come on!" with a whole other intent.

Simply put, when the answer isn't an obvious *yes*, or a flat out, "Hey, can you stop what you are doing?" Then first *stop, stop, stop* and sincerely *apologize*. We all make mistakes, and you'll make a lot more before you're planted in the cold, cold ground, so you might as well get used to owning up to them.

But mean it, okay? Don't just say it to get the other party to shut up. Put yourself in their shoes.

Empathy, remember? And respect!

There's a word, a particular word, for people who don't consent before… well, pretty much ANYTHING involving sex. It's not a magic word like *please* but rather one that could damage another person (even if you didn't mean it to) as well as land you in some equally land you in boiling water. The word is an assault. Touching someone without their permission, especially in a sexual way, is pure and simple assault.

And, just to be extra clear: remember, someone whose judgment is impaired (by substances, mental state, or medical condition), who has been pressured or coerced, or who has been manipulated in any way or who is UNDER THE AGE OF LEGAL CONSENT cannot give explicit consent.

This goes for non-human creatures as well…and please, don't make us spell this particular caution out for you. You get what we are on about here. Humans are the only species that can give consent to other humans and the human giving the consent, again in a multitude of ways it can be given, need be of their right mind when giving it.

Consent, by the way, be rescinded at any time for any reason. No explanations or apologies are needed. *No* means *no*, no matter when it is said. When someone says *no*, stop whatever the hell you're doing.

Yeah, we know you are all worked up and things seem to be going swimmingly. The leather bodices have been ripped off. Naughty utterances have been uttered. All manner of power toys have been charged. But consent means *having the right to be heard when you feel uncomfortable during, well, whatever and the other person hearing you and stopping.*

Are we clear? Are you sure?

You'd damned well better be.

We hate to have to start the glories of our fun sexual how-to (and why not) book with such a cold water bath, but you and us and everyone needs to be clear about consent. Sex is about passion, about desire, about fun, about giggles, about squeals, and (yes) even about love. It can also be about one partner saying, "No, no, no," when they mean "Yes, yes, yes." But sex is also about understanding, compassion, thoughtfulness, sharing—and especially about *empathy* and *respect*.

So go forth and have a sweaty and shaky good time doing whatever turns you on ... just be sure and do it with your eyes and ears wide open and that you ask for, receive, and give explicit consent.

CHAPTER 2:
Yes, Virginia You Can Go Home Again—
But They Have Moved All The Furniture

Living with your lover's sexual past.

It's a reality.

I'm not so sure how naive you are or would admit to being. But do you think your magnificent budding love/sex been carved from virginal stone—just waiting for your oh-so-sexy touch to flower into magnificent sexuality? If you need to kid yourself into believing that all that current bumping, slurping, and tugging you and your shmoopie-bear are engaging in is the very first time your partner has used their sexy bits so ardently, go ahead and delude yourself.

Most probably your partner had a partner or two (or three or a hundred) before your wonderfulness came gracing their way and some of those partners probably made them as excited as you make them. Maybe a few past partners made them even more excited than you. I know, ouch, right? But the fact is you're probably not the biggest your partner has ever seen. Somewhere before you, your lover probably saw/spanked/nuzzled up to other crumpets and muffins that might have been even firmer, tighter, or curvier than yours. Again, ouch, right?

Live with it. You'll sleep better.

But that's the problem, isn't it — seeing if and how you can live with it?

There go your mental wheels spinning over those who have come before you (and when we say 'come,' we do mean come). That hot mind ember of "Who were they with?" and "What did they do with them?" has burrowed itself into your brain and won't let you go, right? We get it. We've been there. Once these thoughts take root they are damn hard to grab out of the fertile ground that is your mind.

Be it with a brand-new lover or someone we may have been married to for years, people too often want to know what they really shouldn't know about their partner, investigate infinitum … want to boldly go where no person should ever go.

But don't fret, we've come to quell your curiosity. We want to stop you from looking back when you should be foraying forward in your making-the-beast-with-two-hindquarters. In what follows, you'll learn how to apply the discipline needed to keep you in the here-and-now of your romantic relationship.

We know precisely how this bugs you and we can certainly lend a hand in how to deal with your partner's past or, more precisely, how to keep it *in the past*.

The past is the unknown. That's what makes it so unknowable.

All those wild imaginings of sexual trysts, the deep heartfelt moments of lust you assume lay in your partner's past glories were not as intense as you fitfully imagine them to be. Sure, just like you, your partner probably had a few knock-out drag-out fuck fests, maybe some stuff they could only ever engage in when they were in their mid-20's and still limber.

But really, we all imagine scenarios that, in the clear light of reality, were never as romantic or as pornographic as our fevered (see: *jealous*) imaginations make them out to be.

Face it, one of the things that gets you all heated-up nutty about your partner's long-ago liaisons is less them mentioning a moment here or there, or even them keeping a picture of the ex (alright, maybe that does bug you) but probably more the fact that you can't put their past in perspective like you can your own.

And you'll never be able to put their past in perspective because it is *not* your own.

We invest extra special meaning to stuff we did not experience. It's the classic fear of the unknown. We also have a tendency, in our attempt to protect our psyche, to do what noted psychologist Dr. Albert Ellis called *awfulizing*: ruminating over something we have yet to do or have never seen and giving it dire connotations.

In this case, it wouldn't be the thing itself that we'd imagine so awful. When we think about our lover way back when having some sexual fun, we tend to ramp it up to be the very best sex they ever had. But imagining the best here 'awfulizes' the moments for us. In our imaginations, what went before has an ever-so-heightened potency. In reality, whatever it was that our partner got into with whomever could never really have been as pornographic as we imagine it to be.

Just put the five-inch stilettos on the other foot.

Think about your long-lost loves or past sexual encounters: the good ones, some great, some not so great. This is most probably the way it is for your lover as well... unless they were exceedingly cursed or lucky or had lots of money to pay for precisely that which they wanted. They weren't porn stars (okay, maybe some of you are indeed in a relationship with a porn star, that will take a whole other kind of discussion) but mostly, the person you are presently with probably had a sex life, give or take, pretty much like yours.

A time machine is not your friend.

Staving off going backward on yourself or your lover (and not 'backward' in the way you think ... you're *such* a reprobate!), is easier said than done. It might be less your slipping self-discipline here than the time machines we all have at our disposal that brings us back time and again, even when we don't want to look back

Facebook, Google and pretty much any other online searching technology make it too damn easy to look up an old ex. It could even be argued that these social media and Internet platforms break-up more couples than any wild drunken one-night stand. It's just way too easy for us to revisit our pasts or map the progress of a partner.

You know the old saying *you can't go home again?* Well, you certainly can. But figuratively speaking, your room has been rented and the furniture sold.

Nothing good will come of traipsing back in time, whether it's you doing it looking to find an ex just to talk with (yeah, right) or chasing after your significant other's sexual ghosts. So, whether you're using Facebook to turn back the years or just your brittle rose-colored imaginings, get out of those time machines when you have the juicy potential of a present you're building with someone.

You're competing with a limited view.

The here and now can't compete with your lover's past fly-in-amber-like moments. Their old stallion-of-a-bed-mate doesn't burp, pick their nose or have a bad hair day. That wonderful person who smelled of lilacs and honey from long ago doesn't utter an opinion, pro or con. That genuinely remarkable person who managed those athletic feats of daring-do in the bedroom doesn't accidentally have you roll over into the wet spot.

Sure, the reality is, your lover's former lovers did all of the above, and probably worse. But when hard-pressed to recall good/great or Earth-rocking sexual canoodles (or looking to piss a new lover off when that new lover keeps push, push, pushing about our sexual past and we just want to shut them up!) you'll find that we all forget the bad stuff. And don't forget you do all of this too when thinking/fantasizing about a past lover.

It's not a deep realistic dive any of us take when we recall the limited view of our past sexual moments. Memory tends to cloud the real stuff. Old flames exist in an otherworldly, incomparable time.

But they ain't here in the here-and-now.

You'll never really know the truth. The answers you seek are not clear.

Keep this last little kernel of possibility close to that burning ember of obsession you can't seem to extinguish. Even if you ask and your lover gives forth answers, they might very well be lying to you about what went on before they came into your life, as much to save your feelings as maybe they are conflating memories, recalling things inaccurately.

Let's take this last point first.

Even in the best of circumstances, with your most vivid past moments, how much of what you remember can you say for one hundred percent certainty is exactly the way things went down? Yeah, yeah, we know, you are among that small percentage of the population with an eidetic memory, you recall every little word spoken, every stroke, every ...

Come on, you know you have those moments when you fill in the blanks as much as you do those when maybe this or that happened on a Tuesday instead of a Friday as you first thought.

The point being — how much of your lover's past memory can you really rely on, especially when you are pushing like a detective for the real truth?

Often, they will even tell you as much. "Hey, that was years ago, I can't remember every single measurement or exactly what chocolate sauce we used."

And, secondly (and this is a hard one to come to terms with when what you are after is the truth, the whole truth and nothing but the truth) to save face, to spare your feelings or simply because they don't want to admit how much they used to love the feeling of a whip in their hands during sex, your lover might out and out lie to you about their past.

Yes, it's been known to happen.

* * * *

In the end, when it comes to dealing with your lover's past, or even your own, the choices are few. Either you let your partner's former love life eat away at you *or you let it go*.

"Who-were-you with?" "How many were you with?" "What exactly did you do when you were with the whole college chess club?" If you head down the road of questioning, you'll never be satisfied — or worse — you might be repulsed by the answers your date/lover/possible-spouse gives you.

If you learn that, God forbid, that your partner has had more experiences than you, that your boy toy has splashed naked in all kinds of pools, that your partner can't even calculate how many bare booties they spanked during their dating life before you but has never once raised a firm hand to your backside or that your live-in playmate, like you, also dated the most sultry and dangerous person in town, your feelings of sexual inadequacy might fester to the point you might doubt yourself more than you do already.

And much, much worse, all this looking to the past can all too easily erode all the good you're feeling in the present with your lover.

So, stop it.

Now!

Okay? Really!

Stop it!

CHAPTER 3:
Come And Knock On Our Door

Negotiating a Ménage À Trois

Looking to add some spark to your monogamous sex life?

Wanting to trip the light fantastic by morphing two into three?

Do you have an itch for making your BFF a wet, warm, and randy BFF for your partner?

Looking to slip between the sheets, and the relationship of a couple you have had your eye on for a while or just for the past few hours?

The *ménage à trois* is a fantasy that lovers giggle over during pillow talk (or that three people might try during a one-time drunken night of neighborly camaraderie). Sometimes the classic threesome is even something that a trio builds on until they are committed polyamorists. In other instances, a *ménage à trois* gives an otherwise monogamous couple a little time off from their traditions.

No matter where you are in a relationship, inviting another person into your bed, or you, the invitee jumping in, the reasons to pursue this unique hook-up could be many.

And although the last thing we would ever want to do is kill your potential good time, we do caution that everyone desiring a *ménage à trois* should proceed carefully–and most of all ask (remember our consent chapter?), if not everyone involved, then at least themselves, some fundamental questions. Simply, you'll want to make sure that what is about to or already might have happened comes off with as few complications as possible.

First and foremost question:

Why are we doing this?

If asking good ole Mary or Frank to go to bed is just something to do on Saturday night, or if you're just lying around with nothing to do with your genitals and you've kinda, well, always thought your best friends were a cute couple, then have at it. But a little talk between the couple and the third is never a bad idea.

In fact, we'd say it's pretty damn important.

Even if everybody is in perfect accord, don't let a little abandon supersede good sense.

Even if everything goes well, and everybody is completely on board, this kind of hooking-up will always fall into one of those "can't unring a bell" moments. You and the people involved might even come to justify it later as

"Well, we were all pretty drunk at the time" (which if you recall is *against one of the fundamental tenets of consent*). So do yourselves a favor and talk this out the best you can before, during, *and* after.

You know the way it often is with fantasies, fetishes, and kinks (and lions and tigers, and bears, oh my!). We've probably all participated in some romping that maybe we weren't so utterly thrilled with simply because we knew it got our lover all hot and bothered, and we enjoyed being the one that got them into that state. You know, you sometimes kinda do stuff, just because...and that's okay. You can't be into every single thing one-hundred percent of the time.

But the old *ménage à tickle* is a different animal.

Even if a threesome (or even a more-some) is something that tickles your interest, you still should give everyone involved, especially yourself, an opportunity to share concerns. Don't just go along providing/asking for this sexual diversion of perversion. Instead, take time to explore the concept before the execution, at least in your mind, what this is all about, and why you want it to happen.

And maybe why you *don't*.

Then listen, rinse, and repeat when the other two folks involved want to talk about their concerns and ideas.

Question two:
Who is your third?

As crucial as exploring the *why* of the threesome is determining *who* you might want to invite into your equation.

Do you pick a stranger or friend?

Inviting a friend to your bed means you'll enjoy a pre-vetted lover between the sheets, somebody you could always share a knowing wink with or another stab at when all three people are feeling randy. This kind of hooking-up gives the term 'best friend' a whole other meaning.

But it also can be erotic as all get out, making it with that sexy, sultry stranger you meet drinking at the beach bar. Just imagine you and your partner going home with the very best "look what (or who) we did on our summer vacation" story. Just be safe and make with the condoms, etc.

Or you could always call in a professional, a person who will know exactly what to do and won't be connected to you or your lover afterward in any way.

And realize please, that even though you and yours might be raring to go, think yourselves to be the hottest, cleanest, most relaxed couple on the block, it could take a while for both of you to agree on a partner and *then* have that person agree to go to bed with both of you.

Question three:
Who Will Be Doing What To Whom?

There are so many mathematical sexual conundrums to this bedscapade that it could leave you more brain-fried than trying to work eighth-grade algebra homework.

For instance: if you're a queer, male-identified couple asking a third man to play with you, the field can be relatively equal.

But what if you want to ask a female-identified person to your bed? And if you do, which one of you is going to take point? Or what if you're a dyed-in-the-wool 100% Catholic Church-abiding person? What's allowed with this third person you aren't married to? Might bringing another sexual partner to your bed impinge on your beliefs?

And for trans-folx, might you have questions about who does what to whom, where, and for how long?

Hell, anybody could have any combination or all of the questions above.

Let's face it, for many the threesome is a one-time or only a few times deal. Partners are looking to explore the experience for all they can, far afield of what they usually enjoy with one another. It may just mean, for this night, one person or partner enjoys some sexual experimentation they don't usually get.

So, what will it be then and for whom?

What to do? Well, the best thing to do, as mentioned above, is to *talk*. Discuss precisely what is and *is not* on the agenda for everyone involved. Knowing beforehand who will be doing what to whom or where/what and the why is never a bad idea.

And yes, you all might not know exactly and some things that happen organically could lead you down a garden path you never thought before about mowing (and by mowing, we mean…). But be sure to discuss those things you *really* want to do, as much as those you do not.

Question four:
Will This Continue–Or Is It A One-Time Thing?

This question might follow directly from "Why are we doing this?"

As mentioned, in various instances, the *ménage à* thingie is a one-time occurrence. Other times, randy friends fall into bed without even knowing it. Okay, they know it, but they don't care how they got there.

Still, at other, *other* times, the single, odd person sweet-talks their married friends into a get-together. But some *ménage à trois* become actual live-in situations, the third not so much making the relationship vehicle wobbly as propagating some sweet polyamorous steering. The jury is still out if we are indeed the kind of animals that flourish or die when it comes to being monogamous, ya know, that one-on-one, two people only ever have sex with each other thing.

But, that being said, there's also a chance that the threesome can cause some things, least of all relationships, to come crashing down. The couple who invite a third to their bed might find this kind of sex play forces a fissure into what was a stable relationship. It's been known to happen. Or maybe the third who comes in exposes too much of themselves or experiences their friends in ways they really never expected and begs out of the longtime friendship after the *ménage*.

Still, Plenty of live-in lovers jumped there from being part of a *ménage à trois*, meaning that there's a real possibility that a *ménage* can be a positive experience in so many ways, one of them seemingly pretty traditional.

The solution to this: everyone needs to communicate and, most of all, feel empowered and comfortable in saying if what's happening should go forward, be paused, or ended *at any time*.

* * * *

This Is The End

As mentioned slightly above, there can come some obstacles to all this juicy three-person goodness.

Many times, the *ménage à trois* overstays its welcome for one or more of the partners. Let's face it, when it comes to sex, we have all been involved in those moments where the flesh is willing, happy, and furiously begging to be satiated at regular intervals that we let our fun bits dictate our actions beyond where our emotions and sensibilities really want to go.

Sure, pushing ourselves can be arousing. We often take pride in doing something even though deep down we aren't in our comfort zone. And then there is the idea of bubbling forth some disappointment from our fellow bed partners if calling *stop* or even just *slow down*. Quite often we'll continue dipping back into a well for a whole host of reasons when given our druthers, we'd rather things would stop. But as we have probably been slowly indicating all throughout this chapter, it's best to end a *ménage à trois* the moment you feel it's not working for you, for whatever reason.

There's no shame in making your point plain and clear here. Again, the other two players, and one even possibly your full-time lover/mate might not want to stop, but doing so, sooner rather than later, when you feel that twinge of "ya know, I'm kinda not into this anymore, sorry" is much better than feeling disempowered, insecure, or doing something for all the wrong reasons.

Remember, just because you might be able to do something doesn't mean you always should.

* * * *

Hopefully, whatever happens in your *ménage à trois* everybody has a good time, and nobody gets hurt. Maybe in the future, when you or your partner feels unusually passionate, you can recall the moment or moments when you had that third person in bed and work some foreplay off of this.

Maybe, too, you like having that little secret with your friend and their partner and will forever manage a wink with the two of them at a party.

And if you haven't rolled the threesome into a lifestyle, there's that remarkable story to tell about when you got tipped so extra special by that sweet sexy couple from Alabama.

Just make sure to go into any trio with your communication lines as open as possible, and bring with you love and respect for each other and anyone else involved as well.

CHAPTER 4:
How To Love Many And Love Them Well

What is Polyam?

Multiple partner intimacy (beyond the *ménage à trois* or swinging) is pretty simple to define but offers a practically infinite amount of variables, styles, and forms.

Simply put…Polyamory (polyam for short) is about being emotionally and/or sexually connected to more than one person at a time.

As for what makes a happy polyam relationship, well, that, too, is simple in concept. So simple that it can be summed up in only a few words:

Are you happy, and is everyone you're involved with happy?

If the answer is yes, then congratulations! Please pick up your complimentary gift basket on the way out. It's when the answer is… shall we say… less than a resounding yes, or less than a violent up and down shake of the head, that some real work needs to begin.

But don't feel bad. Like any relationship, a non-monogamous one has its fluctuations, and rethinking, renegotiating, or reevaluating may happen at any time. Because of this, it's always a good idea to pause every once in a while and check in with all the people involved in a sexual relationship, particularly yourself.

And in that checking-in, one of the most common hurdles people face in a polyamorous relationship is that green-eyed monster. jealousy.

Some polyam people look at jealousy as something to be avoided or defeated. But jealousy is a valid and understandable emotion. It's something that practically every human experiences. Still, this doesn't mean you can look jealousy in its metaphorical face and understand it. A complicated emotion, jealousy often springs from feeling that someone else is getting what you aren't. Specifically, for what we are discussing here, it would be jealousy over the fact that "my partner is taking sex or love away from me and giving it to someone else."

Where the good health of any relationship is built on a bedrock of communication, in a non-monogamy situation, communication is even more critical. As there are more people involved, all partners involved should be checking in with one another from time to time, but don't forget to check in with yourself.

This is where you can face and understand jealousy best by taking the time to examine your feelings. Just saying to yourself or your partners that you're jealous doesn't do a helluva lot. Through introspection and self-analysis, being able to determine that you're feeling insecure and need more or a certain kind of attention is essential to hopefully get past anger-bred insecurities and depression. You can't get past feeling jealous until you understand why you are feeling jealous.

Also, be sure to check your partners' reactions to your feelings. Suppose you do indeed feel that green-eyed monster (if you didn't know it, jealousy is often called the green-eyed monster, which really put a negative light on those monsters out there running around with that color eye or eyes....we apologize) rising within you and come to share this feeling with the person or people you're involved with, and you sense, or outright know, that you're not being respected, heard, or maybe you're even mocked. In that case, it might be time to have a serious discussion with your polyam partners. Or it might even mean these non-monogamous partners can no longer be your polyam partners.

No one should ever tell you that you're wrong for feeling jealous. Period.

If the people you share your life and bed with invalidate your feelings or don't even want to talk about your feelings, um, well, they might just not be the people you should be around. That isn't to say that being angry, irrational, or playing emotional games is fair to your partners, either. It's fine and dandy to say you're feeling that you're not getting what other people are, to express the how and why of your jealousy, and to want to have your concerns heard.

But manipulating your partners over unsaid feelings or holding grudges, etc., is not the way to go. Throwing dishes as well as insults, doesn't work so well either. It's a rare person who responds positively to this kind of brutish, bratty behavior. Try to understand your feelings, and bring them with either suggestions or concrete needs to the polyam table. Be honest, talk stuff out, your partners and your own psyche will thank you for it in the long run

And, again, if you do all this correctly, safely and sanely air your feelings and your non-monogamous partners don't respond with compassion and understanding, then it might be time to take a step back and look at what's happening.

Ask yourself: *Are you happy?* If you are not, explore why and address it.

How To Get Into Polyamory

The cold hard truth is the journey of polyam can be as much filled with the best times as well as some terrible ones. Let's face it, two people trying to finagle their way through a relationship is hard enough. Add another person into the mix, or even a fourth, the possibilities for some wild rough-water-relationship-rafting increase exponentially the more folx you add into your mix. We saw this when just dipping-a-toe (or whatever else) into the waters of the *ménage à trois*; polyam is multiple-partnering on a whole other level.

With very few exceptions, most cultures don't provide a societal roadmap for this way of living. Monogamy/ Sure, that's easy! Date, marry, move in, have kids ... blah, blah, blah.

But non-monogamy? Nope.

That's why it's essential to give yourself plenty of love and get lots of support. Try and understand that you're taking a courageous step when opening yourself up to loving more than one person at a time.

Now, getting into polyam has as many paths as there are non-monogamous combinations. But, for the sake of simplicity, we are going to focus on two.

The first is going from a monogamous relationship to an open one. For most people, it's kind of an all-or-nothing situation from discussing it, planning for it, and then jumping in with both feet. The absence of, for lack of a better term, training wheels, can result in two extremes. Couples either suddenly realize that polyam is the life for them (as in, non-monogamy where have you been all my life?) or they run screaming for the hills.

After all, talking about playing sexually with someone else in addition to your primary partner longer than maybe for one night of switch and swinging revelry is one thing. Doing it is quite another.

It's a good idea to take this all really, really, really slowly, especially if you're feeling nervous. Everyone's path is different. What might work for you won't work for someone else (even your new partners). For instance, instead of leaping into bed in your various combinations, what about spending some time paired up in those combinations engaged in sensual but not sexual activities, or even in mundane ones. That way, you can see how you all feel about one another without the (fun) distractions of sex.

And, naturally, keep on keeping those lines of communication open. If you like to chat on the phone, then do that. If you prefer to sit down face-to-face, then that's the ticket. Maybe email or texting is your cup of tea? Whatever works for you and the people you're involved with, just keep talking as much as you keep doing everything else. If you're "going polyam," you will have to know how to make it work in the clear light of day when you're all just doing pretty much everyday, run-of-the-mill, get-through-your-life boring stuff.

Another entry into the world of non-monogamy is through BDSM. The significant benefit to this is that BDSM can have lots of training wheels moments. Going to BDSM events, playing with other people (though not always sexually) can be an excellent place to try out how polyam feels. You can literally work out in real-time those moments where feelings of jealousy might appear.

Be cautioned here, though.

One of the most common challenges that can come from getting into polyam through BDSM stem from those who participate in domination/submission power dynamics. Top and bottom roles may get in the way of communication, especially for those who are inexperienced with expressing their needs. Thus, it is advisable for everyone involved to discuss and negotiate the structure of being non-monogamous outside of a BDSM relationship and put aside roleplay roles now and again to check in with everyone involved. Bottoms and tops can be polyam, certainly, but one doesn't always spawn the other or vice versa.

Some people in the BDSM scene might begin to feel that being polyam is somehow mandatory to being kinky. True, non-monogamy can be quite prevalent in the BDSM world, but it is by no means a hard and fast rule that if you are into BDSM, you need to be polyam. Back to our maxim: *are you happy?*

If you're kinky and non-monogamous (and you know it, clap your hands), but not content, then it might be time to make some changes.

There are lots of happy, *monogamous* people in the BDSM world. If you are being told that you're not up to kink standard for being with just one person, this is as much not okay as it isn't the truth.

As for locating polyam-friendly people, the good news is that various sources put the number of people in or having experimented with non-monogamy at one in every five folx.

Yes, you read that right, one in five.

Dating sites like OkCupid and a few others have joined the Polyam Party, allowing people to note on their profiles that they prefer polyamorous partners in their particular searches. There are also polyam support organizations, such as The Polyamory Society, LoveMore, PolyInfo, and dating sites like Polymatchmaking.com, openminded.com, polyamory.dating.com, plus many others.

While non-monogamy has been gaining acceptance, it doesn't mean that there still aren't people who wouldn't condemn you for trying to open yourself emotionally and sexually. Because of this, be careful about what you share on social media. One wrong post on Facebook and you have outed yourself to people you may not have wanted to know of your status.

A quick word of advice in regards to online dating in this world, in general. Sadly, many people will respond to your profile that they are indeed open to, or curious about, polyam. Not to throw a net over every one of these people, but there's a big difference between being interested and being an active polyamorous person. One thing you don't want to do is become involved with a person who was just looking for so-called easy sex or a way to separate you from your other partner(s). But if you do find someone you like who doesn't have direct polyam experience, it might be a good idea to take it rrreeeaaalllyyy ssslllooowww until you have a feeling that they genuinely understand what non-monogamy means.

Now, for the various forms polyam can take. Not to repeat, repeat, repeat ourselves yet again, but as long as the people involved are happy, the variables, styles, and forms can be absolutely anything.

Quick examples: a couple in an open marriage, where it's agreed that both can have as many lovers as they like, as long as both spend a majority of time together; the BDSM triad of top, bottom, and another bottom; group scenes where everyone gets together on Sunday mornings to make pancakes; a couple that can have other lovers, but only when traveling away from home; an individual who prefers not to be coupled but, instead, have a circle of lovers who may, or may not, be aware of each other.

Polyamory is whatever you and your non-monogamous partners think up, even if woefully unconventional, even in the unconventional polyam world, determines the parameters of the polyam life you're living. For instance, some non-monogamous people expect their partner, or partners, to tell them everything and anything. For others, the out of sight/out of mind axiom suits them better. For this latter group, meeting a playmate or lover would be stressful. For the former, this is how partners put a face to a name so as not to allow their imaginations to run to dark places.

* * * *

In the end, let's go back to the beginning. No matter how many people are involved, whatever your determined degree of sharing, the amount of sex or kinky play involved, and how much partners reveal to one another, the bottom-line health mandate of a polyam relationship is built on two things:

Is everyone in the relationship, meaning you *and* your partners, happy?

And, do not judge what you do (or don't do) by the standards of anyone else.

Actually, this second point should apply to all of life, no? As in, 'tend your own garden, and don't be distracted by anyone else's weeds.'

While non-monogamy is not an easy road, and rough patches are all but guaranteed, when it goes well, it can be a fantastic experience to open your life to loving many people, emotionally as well as sexually, and, best of all, loving them really, *really* well.

CHAPTER 5:
Lip Service

Cunnilingus for the Clueless

There's not a lot of middle ground when it comes to cunnilingus. You either like licking/eating pussy, or you don't.

And as we all know, the key to doing something well is having a desire to do that thing.

Now, for lots of vagina-equipped people, while fucking is undoubtedly fun, orgasm only comes through clitoral stimulation. Therefore, that little point needs to be approached creatively.

Yes, fingers work, and vibrating toys can get the job done. But you'll hear many vulva-owners asking for their lover's tongue, nose, and/or lips down there more often than not. It merely is that thing that they can't give themselves (unless the person in question is a contortionist of the highest order) and that which provides just the right soft attention that many a person prefers.

And really, you want to be doing this correctly, or not doing it at all if you don't want to. But, if you don't want to, you might find it very hard finding a person who is perfectly content with your 'no cunnilingus' policy (the act of one person performing oral sex on a vagina) it may impact your chances of finding a partner who'll return the oral sex favor.

So, let's assume you want to. Then how do you do it correctly? How do you know what every vulva-owner might want down there when we know every vagina is as individual as a snowflake?

And as pretty, right?

What's more, how do we get past the myths and worries that everyone apparently has about this particular flavor of oral sex?

This prompts a point we think (mentioning here, now and forever) regarding sex and techniques…mainly that no one can give another person an orgasm. You can work on/with/under them (and for our purposes here, it would be the vagina-equipped person having the orgasm). But, in the end, it's the receiver's mind with the help of your hands, lips, tongue or toy that results in deliciously happy noises, times, and fluids.

Sex is sharing, a partnership of two people making beautiful music together (or more than two, you lucky bugger!) with emotions, mental and physical stimulation, and a whole lot of libido stimulation. But never forget, the person shaking, rattling, and rolling themselves to an orgasm only gets there because they have the desire to come.

Okay, now back to licking...

Stop, Look And...

Aficionados of cunnilingus often think that loving a vagina's flavor instantly gives them super pussy-licking powers. But just liking something doesn't mean that you're particularly good at it. Yes, as mentioned before, it goes a long way to be into this activity to do it well, but remember, just because you dance a mean groove to Bach, Beethoven, and/or The Beatles doesn't mean you can carry a tune.

So, even though you think you may know and have tried every little nibble, flicker, kiss, lick, suck, or blow (and please, never blow into a vagina...that's a big no no), this doesn't mean you should be walking around sporting such a satisfied smirk.

Even a maestro should learn to play more than one tune.

The difference between serenading your lover with a cheap harmonica instead of a Stradivarius is not always easy to manage. (Yeah, yeah, they are two different instruments. Don't be so picky, you'll miss the point.) The point is, it can be a mighty dark and mysterious world when you face someone in this particular way, akin to playing Black Jack late at night at an abandoned fuzzy felt casino table, with no dealer insight to give you even the smallest prompt of when to fold or take a hit. But if you don't want to look like you're auditioning for a jug band rather than the Met, (sorry about overdoing the music metaphors), there are some techniques you can use to increase your confidence. Like a lot of making yourself dynamite in bed tricks, these are hardly guaranteed, but these may help you get over your nerves, so you won't whine like an idiot across your partner's labia when you next go to kiss them between the thighs.

First and foremost, anyone who wants to give cunnilingus a shot should scope out the territory. While it's true that every vulva and vagina is different, there's still often similarities among those with them: labia majora (big lips, on the outside), labia minora (small lips, on the inside), urethra (near the top), vaginal orifice (pretty much dead center), anus (at the bottom) and clitoris (at the very top).

Too many have regretfully ignored the clit.

"Obviously!" We hear a lot.

It's just crucial to realize there's a lot more down there.

And sometimes, a person may have some differences that their partner has never seen. A person with a vagina may have a medical condition known as pelvic organ prolapse where the rectum, uterus, or bladder may have "dropped" into the vagina, and so the interior may look and feel different. If you encounter this, please do not shame a partner. They are often embarrassed enough already. There may also be pelvic pain associated with this condition. Be compassionate and ask for information.

The entire genital area can be sensitive, a delightful, erotic playground for everyone concerned. Before parting the labia and burying your face between thighs though, take some time to look where you're going. Use your fingers (gently, please) to see exactly what's where, but make this less a clinical examination and more a loving appreciation.

Aside from spread-eagles in magazines and on Clips4Sale downloads, when's the last time you took a good, long look at a pussy? They're quite pretty, you know: pinks and reds, tan and even purple, sometimes. Georgia O'Keefe thought they were gorgeous enough to paint and hang on walls. (If you think she was drawing flowers, we have some beach-front property in Kansas, we;d love to sell you) .

So, look before you taste, and don't go leaping right after that oh-so-alluring clit. Take your time before you insert, lap at, or suck with tongue and lips. The clit is undoubtedly a big ON button for the labia-equipped, but it's not the only way to get someone's motor started.

Find out by doing.

Does the person who owns this va-gay-jay like to be kissed down there, everywhere, both hard and softly? Do they like to have their lips gently sucked? Might they enjoy a fingertip eased in as you lick? Maybe they want the attention of more than one finger (and more than just the tip) and perhaps not only in the vagina … *wink wink.*

Come on, take some time to touch while you look, and also—

Listen

How will you know whether your efforts are working? Well, duh, *ask!*

If you're nervous, just query your partner if there's anything they like or don't. Keep the Q & A as brief as possible, though. You might be able to even make it into a sex game. But getting intel about what works here, from the person who happens to own the vagina you're going down on, is better than trying everything and hoping that something will work. After all, this is about oral sex, and the best oral tool for pleasing a person is to open your mouth and ask your partner what they do or don't like, before, during, and after you lick.

There's a lot more to communication though than the words we speak.

Some people are too shy to tell you what they want or don't know how to articulate what pleases them. It's your job to take your listening skills to a whole new level, no matter how vocal (or not) your partner might be. If they aren't vocal with instructions or letting fly with the exclamations, listen to the sounds they're making (or not making).

'Listen' to movement, too.

If suddenly the person you are kissing in this most intimate of ways is slapping their booty on the bed, if their body is quivering and quaking, as if they are enduring seism-orgasmic shock waves as you lap, you might want to regard this all as a good thing. The same is true for the moans, coos, sighs, hisses, and other various happy noises you have heard them make before and are hopefully making them make again when you go down on them.

Just be ready for some new sounds and shimmies, if this is the first time you're visiting down south. Or even if you have been down on this muffin before and you suddenly change your lapping speed or technique. You just never know, and that's the fun of all of this sex stuff; discoveries are possible at all times.

The Surgeon General Recommends

As with all sex, it's best you understand the risks involved with licking pussy. Sorry, folx, it's time for another lesson in the realities of sex in these perilous times. While the verdict is still out on HIV transmission, through oral sex, there's always the big bad hepatitis C lurking. Very easy to catch, hepatitis C can mean anything from a lifetime with a debilitating illness to ending up on a liver transplant list.

Luckily, the usual precautions for hepatitis also work against most other sexually transmitted conditions like HIV, gonorrhea, and other nasty bugs. One of the best is the barrier method, using plastic wrap between the mouth and vagina. It might look silly, wrapping your partner in non-porous material, but it'll keep any potential microscopic troublemakers away when you're sharing that most intimate of kisses.

The best prevention, though, is information. Use your brain as well as your genitals or mouth during sex. In short, be picky about who you go down on. Sex is about trust and sharing. So how can you have a good time when you don't feel safe with someone?

For peace-of-mind, get tested for HIV, hep C, and herpes. If you don't know your partner's health status, then treat them as if they were positive for everything. If you want to know more about sexually transmitted conditions and safer sex, check out San Francisco Sex Information (www.sfsi.org) or hep C alert (www.hep-c-alert.org).

This all might sound a bit alarmist, but it's a lot better than living with a lifetime of discomfort or even not living at all. Play safe, play smart, and be around long enough to play a lot.

Diving In

Back to your time between the legs.

After you've taken a good–and most importantly, an appreciative–look at your partner's pussy, found out all you can about them and paid attention to what they're saying (spoken or not), then you can get to it.

Cunnilingus is akin to a French kiss.

Think about that for a moment. When you're locked in a passionate embrace, you're not just tongue dancing. There are lips as well as other fun mouth bits involved. The same should be true when licking your lover. You don't want to be a sloppy lapper. Think of what you're doing as giving your partner a good Frenchie between the legs.

Depending on your lover, leaping right in is not always the best way to go. Like a kiss, cunnilingus should be something you do together to stoke your fires. Start slowly, start playfully, and even laugh a lot. Even if things are especially hot and heavy between two folx, approaching the clit can sometimes be a bit too intense. Start by gently parting the labia so you know what's where.

This is where an appreciative eye comes in. Look at the colors, the shape of the lips, the size of the clit. Run your fingers and tongue along the major and minora, or gently insert a finger into the vaginal opening and circle the inner muscle. Some people will lubricate very early, while others need more time or stimulus. You can also sometimes see the muscles of the vagina contract and release as you touch and lick.

It's quite an erotic sight.

After you've used your eyes and fingers to explore the genital contours of your lover, it's time for a kiss. Try licking around, above, or below the clit, applying some gentle pressure, pushing with your tongue rather than lapping in weak, flaccid strokes.

When it comes time to approach the clit, one of the most important things to remember is consistency. An erratic, spasmodic approach will usually get you nothing but a smack across the top of the head. Breaking up your licking into slow and fast spurts is a good idea, if anything, to avoid monotony. Though before doing anything please check in with your partner first.

If you're jumping all over the place, in either speed or location, you're not going to give your partner a chance to focus enough on orgasm. It's a good idea to develop a comfortable frequency (fast, firm licks, for instance) followed by a low period (where you can breathe and rest your tongue). Listen to their responses and stick with a rhythm that works for both of you.

Stiffness is equally essential. Few people like to have a warm, soft slab dragged across their clits, so keep your tongue firm and tight, like a fingertip, as you flick it across and around the clit. But don't go in as if you're trying to work a spot off that pleasure point!

Moisture usually isn't much of a problem in cunnilingus, but there's an art to keeping the clit moist but not too wet. A few strategic swallows can do wonders for a balance between the two.

Remember, you don't have to depend on tongue power entirely. So, too, if you get tired, need a break, or need to see where the hell you're licking, take a break. Remember, using your finger or a sex toy is perfectly okay.

Besides your tongue or fingers, consider your nose or chin as well (but be careful of that razor stubble).

As with sex in general, being comfortable and engaged in the experience is key to both of you having a good time. You don't have to be a cunnilingus purist. Licking your lover should be just one of the things you can do. Rather than just licking and licking and licking 'til you both get bored, try mixing and matching it with other types of sex play.

And don't lose sight of the fact that not everyone can orgasm from oral sex, no matter if you're an Olympic-level licker. That doesn't mean their partner doesn't enjoy it, just that they might need an extra hand, finger, or vibrator to help them peak.

This is where we get back to communication.

Be flexible and responsive to what you both need to have a good time. Talk, play, and experiment to find out what works for you and what works for your partner!

Practicing When Not Down On It

Believe it or not, there are ways to prepare to perform for cunnilingus. No, you're not going to find a pussy-eating machine at the gym, but there are some exercises any one of us could engage in to make us better at this beautiful activity.

1) Eat any single-serve Jell-O, pudding, etc., cup *without utensils or your hands*. This is an excellent way to get down deep into a wet spongy surface and better your skills. Plus, in this case, you extract some yummy contents via only your tongue and lips.

2) Try the Lifesaver tip-of-the-tongue strengthening trick. Place a Lifesaver in your mouth, poke the tip of your tongue through its hole, and by circling the tip of your tongue, dissolve the candy from the inside out. This will strengthen your tongue for other uses (and Lifesavers taste so good).

3) Change the way you think about cunnilingus by integrating it into your current erotic fantasies. Do this enough, and soon you will look forward to it. As with many kinds of sex acts, anticipation plus excitement equals a passionate and pleasurable experience.

The Dreaded Question Of Scent

Many have gotten more than their fair share of heartbreak over "the smell." And really, let's stop using that word, okay? The *scent* a healthy vagina generally exudes is an aphrodisiac for anyone who wants to visit down there. In defense of the occasional person whose resistance to cunnilingus is still fueled by, shall we say, issues of fragrance, it's a simple fact of human biology that all kinds of things can affect one's scent and taste.

Most anything off-putting, though, can pretty much be wiped away by a quick bath or a few swipes with a washcloth.

The same way semen can taste from salty to bitter to sweet depending on what the penis owner had for dinner the night before, a pussy can taste/smell different if they eat such things as garlic or specific vitamins.

If there's a continuing problem with smell and taste, try suggesting a change in diet. If the pungency is especially powerful, the person in question might be experiencing some change in the southern climes due to infection.

Yes, there are those times that we have all gone nose blind to our own scents, but the longer you're with a partner, the easier it is to discuss the intricacies of our humanness. Skirt delicately around the question of what you're smelling and why you might be smelling it, but we are all adults here. We can address these issues maturely and sensitively, right?

Be aware of your hygiene, as well. As we mentioned, those sporting a five o'clock shadow may irritate a partner's inner thighs or labia. Think about how you'd feel if a scruffy face foraged around amid your privates!

And don't forget, the mouth is much dirtier than the vagina. So before leaping between those thighs, remember your lunch and what remains of it on your teeth could adversely affect them.

After all, it's polite to be clean and conscientious with your partner and for them to be the same.

* * * *

This is an excellent time to return to our original musical metaphor: having the desire to play this gig, and knowing one end of your instrument from the other, are both essential to a good performance. BUT it's even more important to realize that there is an audience out there (*up* there in most cases) and you need to make sure they are enjoying your concert as much as you enjoy performing it.

So, take some of these techniques, try them out, and remember that it's not the instrument or the song (or person) played but all of them, together, that combine to make beautiful music.

CHAPTER 6:
Handee Dandy Play

The Lost Art Of The Handee

It honestly seems the hand-job has been left on the back burner in our bag of tricks. As the red-headed stepchild of sexual activities, the idea of manual stimulation of the penis leads to age-old conundrums like: "Well, you can do that to yourself, why do you need me to do it to you?" or "Really, my hand's getting tired, can you please come already?"

With this in mind, should we forget the primary pleasure of the handee? Shouldn't we cultivate insight and accuracy as much with our digits as we do every other part of us?

While there is undoubtedly a version of the handee that works for the vagina-equipped, for the purposes of this chapter, we're expounding on the lost art of the hand-job as it applies (or as it is applied) to a penis, a trick as much for steering as to coax, to alight interest or bring on a tug-o'-ecstasy, a hands-on treatise to being hands-on to a cock.

A sexual classic

People have been giving hand-jobs since the beginning of human history. It's simple, easy, and can be done about any place without having to worry about getting the back of someone's head stuck under the steering wheel. Or pinned in the chariot, depending on how far back in history you want to take this.

In general, people-with-penises can touch themselves as much as they want, but not many can suck themselves (except a few celebrities who will remain nameless unless you send us money). But the hand-job is usually more arousing and always fun when commenced by a hand not one's own.

The hand-job is also the second cousin to mouth-on-penis contact.

Because people can touch themselves…they do. (Groan, yes I know that's an old joke.) But it makes sense, of course, that this self-tickle ability makes the hand-job something we seek less from a partner or that they come to regard as less thrilling to deliver.

But neither need be the case.

Then, too, we have all been privy to bad press about hand contact. Phrases like *manual release*, two words placed together in a way that sounds more like a car that's lost its emergency brake, *happy ending*, and *rub and tug* have entered the social lexicon pretty much as pejoratives.

Why?

Well, a lot of it probably has to do with how masturbation continues to freak people out — we would dare say, even more than the kinkiest of partner sex acts. Which is 100 percent silly, as masturbation, with a partner or by yourself, is completely healthy, extremely satisfying, and can help us understand our bodies and sexuality like very little can.

And how better to pass a few minutes?

Championing The Hand

How do we change things so the hand-job can be regarded in the same way as a good old-fashioned blowie? Might we simply call for a day, a week, a month even of world-wide jerking off (if we could get off our fucking smartphones long enough to get the world off in one global, sexual spree?) Or maybe we should all take a breath, sit back, and pause before going south with our hands.

No one is suggesting we give-up our other fun parts or forget the skills we've developed to have fun with them. Instead, communicate with your partner about what they like, what you're comfortable doing, and make beautiful music from then on.

And if it be with your hand, then venture forth with those digits, we say.

So, how to do it?

First and foremost, rid your mind of any agenda. Touching, tickling, and tugging a cock can as much be a means to an end as it can be foreplay.

Whether using oil, spit, or just some well-placed friction, when you do shake hands with a penis, make sure you're doing so with some conviction. Your seeming attention will pay dividends, to be sure. As with what we mentioned in licking pussy, if you don't really want to be handling a penis, then you probably won't handle it all that well.

Now, if you happen to be adept enough that you do bring your partner off (even if that wasn't your specific intention), do them and yourself a favor and please don't scold an unplanned ejaculation, unless that's something you're both into. We should always feel complimented when our partner feels so much pleasure from us that they climax. And actually, if your partner is too-quick-on-the-draw, then a hand-job may be perfect for teaching them, and you, how to slow down.

Or it may be the opposite concern, they don't come and here, with practice, your partner could feel comfortable enough to orgasm in your presence.

Take note: Intimacy can be a significant component of the happy handee. In fact, it could be argued that the hand-job might be about as intimate as you're going to get with your partner. Sure, placing a cock in your mouth is pretty gosh-darned personal. No one will argue that lovers bumping pretties are about as close as two humans can get. But it doesn't compare with lying next to your partner, whispering all manner of naughtiness to them, watching their reactions while manipulating their southern region.

Specific techniques to try?

There are so many a whole book could be written just on this subject alone (might we refer you to Chris and Ralph's next sex tome, *The Band Of The Hand: 101 Hand-job Techniques For Fun and Profit* coming to a bookstore near you-(kidding, this book doesn't exist, though now we are thinking it rightly should). But as you've no doubt realized by now, each cock is its own individual.

As with blowjobs, paying attention to the neighboring environs (testicles, inner thighs, and even anus) can lead the penis-equipped to nirvana, just as there are those who like a slow, cautious dry rub. And just as some people want an entire, clutched tight, fist around them, there'll be others getting off on a finger on either side of their penis head squeezing and moving with the gentlest of movements.

Want to prolong things?

Vary your speed and torque, and every now and again, give a gentle tug to your playmate's balls. The farther you can separate 'the boys' from pulling up to the body when they're growing tight through arousal, the longer you can keep the person who owns that cock from a fount.

* * * *

Really, all the little tricks, techniques, and teasing morsels you come to learn when executing handees across the world's penis population are a piece of the overall puzzle of why a hand-job can be oh so fun and wickedly intimate. So, listen to each partner you touch, read about handees on the 'net, watch some movies and experiment. Just don't go pulling into the good night, There is more to the hand-job than just a solid tug.

CHAPTER 7:
Blow-By-Blow

A Guide To Fellatio

The way to a penis-equipped person's heart, the old adage goes, is through their stomach.

But the *real* way to reach someone who has a penis is to explore them a bit lower down *with your mouth*.

Below we provide people with penises and those who love to gobble them a guide to the most intimate pleasures.

How Can I Get My Partner to Go Down on Me?

We have the inside scoop that one of the most-asked questions from callers to the San Francisco Sex Information switchboard is:

"How can I get my partner to go down on me?"

Alas, there's no simple answer.

The world would be a beautiful place (and a very busy one) if all sex partners had an equal interest in fellatio (the technical term for putting a penis in one's mouth) or cunnilingus. But life doesn't work that way. Sometimes you just have to accept no for an answer. If your partner finds oral sex unappealing, hours of pleading won't work.

Proceed as you will.

But as we mentioned in the chapter before, if someone doesn't like going down on you, they really have no right to complain if you don't reciprocate.

But remember, there's a big difference between begging and discussing.

If your lover shows reluctance, talk about what's bugging them. Who knows, maybe your partner is harboring performance anxieties that you can help assuage.

Often, people shy away from fellatio for very specific (and easily remedied) reasons. The most obvious is the fear of having something rammed down one's throat or getting a load of semen into one's mouth when one least expects or welcomes it.

Don't forget— and reassure— that fellatio doesn't have to mean deep penetration. It can just as easily consist of kisses, licks, and gentle lapping and lovingly sucks up, down, and around the entire penis, just as much as it could mean the giver wanting to execute a full-on hobnobbing and gurgling their partner's come....as not.

As with everything else, communication is vital here to what the giver and getter want.

A little "I am gonna come" from the receiver or gently tapping the shoulder of the giver goes a long way. And approaching giving head as the end of an intimate encounter as much as just foreplay, without an agenda, might just see you begin to enjoy giving.

Take Me To Funkytown

Ah, cleanliness.

Honestly, who'd want to put their mouth on anyone who hadn't taken a few minutes to bathe or trim? Receivers, at the very least be freshly showered if you know a B.J. is imminent (or any sexual play, really). Even a quick wipe with a warm, wet cloth, (soap and water both please!) as washing thoroughly before you meet your partner will pay dividends.

Uncircumcised penises sometimes have a gummy, white build-up under the foreskin, charmingly named "smegma." A gentle wash beforehand will get rid of this. And a little self-grooming (trimming your public hair) will also prove to the one about to get up close and personal with you that you took the time to consider their feelings (and their comfort).

Look, we're animals, pure and simple. We smell. We sweat. Our body hair can retain odor or be prickly against a lover's face. Be mindful of hygiene.

As a side note, when preparing for an assumed blowie, steer clear of applying cologne or anything but non-scented, mild soap. Not only do scented products taste icky but many are extremely allergic to them. The wrong scented substance could cause asthma attacks and an extreme reaction can lead to the emergency room instead of your happy place.

Practice Makes Perfect

So, you're clean and sweet-smelling. Your partner can hardly wait to take the plunge. Are you good to go?

Probably.

But don't forget for those first few times with somebody new, you're going to have to communicate a good deal as you both experiment and play.

The old adage "practice makes perfect" applies here.

Like many skills, fellatio is absolutely improved by practice and positive feedback. The giver should try different techniques, work on new approaches, and be open to instructions. The getter can be vocal, too. In fact, they damn well should be!

The recipient of such unselfish attention must know their body, articulate what they like, and offer praise when their partner does an exceptional job. Compliments not only let people know that they're doing something right but also make them feel good. Even anticlimactic encounters warrant positive feedback. Some people simply do not have orgasms from oral sex (yes, it's true), which might frustrate a giving-it-their-all-until-they-get-lockjaw partner.

But even if a person doesn't achieve orgasm from oral sex, they might nonetheless get an incredible thrill from being on the receiving end of someone who really enjoys this particular kind of giving. The getter should be vocal about the pleasure they are getting and clue their giver into the fact that, though loving what's happening, they don't readily come from it.

Everybody In The Pool

An important factor in performing good fellatio is knowing the primary pleasure spots on the penis. There's also a knack to knowing the corresponding fun zones down there and how to take to them with a little variety. Penises can be tricky critters, as can the surrounding environs. Depending on the person, there can be hot spots of arousal or cold spots that dampen the mood. Lots of things can cause pleasure and/or discomfort. For giver and getter, both a little awareness of sensitivities will pay dividends here.

In circumcised penises, where the foreskin has been removed, the corona (the ridge that runs around the head of the penis) can be very sensitive. In those who still have their foreskins, the head of the penis tends to be sensitive. You may have to work differently around a cut cock than you do around an uncut one.

The urethra (the opening in the tip of the penis where semen and urine come out) is another contentious spot. Some enjoy having this area stimulated, while others can't stand it. Similarly, responses range from happy to horrified at the thought of having testicles squeezed, tickled with a tongue, or "mmm"ed.

For some, every part of their genitals is sensitive from the head of the penis to the base of the scrotum (the ball sack for those of you who prefer more descriptive terms). You can try different sensations all over that territory: gentle squeezes, pulls, sucks, and scratches. Just don't expect every person to react the same way to all your usual tricks.

The key here is to involve as much of your partner's southern region as they like, with as much of yourself as you're comfortable employing. Licking the inner upper thighs, circling the tip of your finger into their anus (please ask before pressing forward here, or at least read well their responses by tickling around the area to see if they are amiable to insertion), rubbing or licking or even pushing a knuckle into their taint—that springy hammock-y bugger-of-an-area right below the balls and the bottom of the crack of their ass—with a light or intense kneading, can work wonders.

Remember, you have fingers, hands, a nose, and a chin. You can even introduce toys while blowing. Variety in what you use, how you use it, and where you use it to build, subside, tease, ignore, and "eat" with abandon is key to keeping fellatio interesting for both parties.

Just listen well for their reactions or actual words of what they like—or don't.

Going To Town When Going Down

Part of the mystique surrounding fellatio is the supposed Holy Grail of deep-throating. Many people feel a terrible sense of frustration when they can't achieve this deep oral nirvana with their lover's chode. But what so many of us fail to realize is that we have been unduly influenced by modern-day porn films, where extra-hung studs gag their willing cock-sucker so much that the sucker has saliva issuing forth, their gulping all but the soundtrack of the scene. This downloadable intel leaves many a person with a dick and the person wanting to suck it thinking that the best blowie has to be one where there is gagging and saliva spurting tsunami-like from the giver's lips, the getter writhing in ecstasy fucking their giver's throat.

Whether you think this is the right way to go— whether you are giver or receiver, sometimes problems stem from a simple lack of compatibility between partners and the reality of giving head (a slang term for blowjob). But we all can't all do what we see in porn.

And who would want to?

The old cliché that "size doesn't matter" disintegrates when it comes to fellatio. If you are indeed hoping to comfortably deep-throat a partner, the size of both mouth and penis need to be compatible for taking off the whole hog.

Think of it this way: putting a big penis in a small mouth is a little like trying to squeeze into a pair of jeans that fit you five years ago. It's not easy or fun, to say the least, and sometimes it's not even possible!

And, it's a bad look.

But one can learn tricks and techniques for taking a penis far down into one's throat, be this something one wants.

Don't eat beforehand and practice this technique when your stomach is empty. Slowly stick your finger down your throat. When you begin to choke, stop, leaving your finger at the gag point. Close your eyes and take a deep breath. When the discomfort has subsided, begin again. Part of learning not to gag is getting used to having something in the back of your throat and knowing you will still be able to breathe.

Over time, you might grow to be a deep throat-er with the best of them.

And the fluid?

Well, we will get to swallowing below (something we wouldn't recommend with a causal partner), but if you both dig lots of cream with your coffee, or just copious amounts of spit— hey go for it, we say. But not everyone takes to such an overabundance of fluids, no matter what kind of fluids they are.

Coping with Condoms

Let's face it. These are not safe times, as we have warned plenty here. Many sexually transmitted infections are spread through oral-genital contact: syphilis, gonorrhea, and herpes to name a few.

The jury is still out about the risk of oral transmission of HIV, the virus that causes AIDS. That does not mean that it's safe to thrust forward or suck unprotected, though. It merely means that the folx in the know doesn't know.

The threat is supposedly lessened if you don't have any cuts or open sores in your mouth and don't swallow semen.

But, frankly, why take the risk?

Unless you're in a monogamous sexual relationship where both partners get regularly tested for infections and only share fluids ("fluid bonded"), please, use condoms.

Condoms need not kill the joy of oral sex. Many people find the rubbery taste unpleasant, but lots have managed to eroticize latex's smell and taste. Use trial and error to find a brand you like. While great for intercourse, lubricated condoms often have a nasty flavor. They can even numb the mouth. They are best avoided for oral sex.

And be cautioned, there are plenty of folx out there allergic to latex, but there are brands of condoms out there made of other materials.

We all have to consider safe sex nowadays to live well. Be prepared, be knowledgeable, and respect both the person you're playing with and yourself.

* * * *

As with everything else we have been talking about in these chapters, how much pleasure you get out of fellatio depends on how much you enjoy it. If you're going down on your partner's egg-roll but only come to lick, kiss, and regard it with the smallest amount of enthusiasm, they are going to notice. Nothing will turn a person off quicker than feeling their partner is doing something out of a sense of duty, duress, or once-a-year for their birthday.

Remember, a blowjob is just another aspect of making love—with all the trust and communication that should come with it.

CHAPTER 8:
The Person With The Most Toys Wins

The Modern Day Adult Toy Market

A long time ago, there was one kind of sex toy: the type that penetrated. Dildos, the toy most used for this penetration, have been around as long as, well, pretty much as long as we've been around. Humans have always had orifices, and we always seemed to have the need to fill them.

With the advent of mechanical engineering and then electricity, we added a new kind of sex toy to those that penetrated: ones that vibrated.

When you look at sex toys today, those are the two basic types... more or less. There are others, to be sure. You can find those that gently constrict and so amplify (like cock rings), those that imitate (like false pussies and plastic tits), those that restrict (like bondage toys or clamps), and the whole world of BDSM playthings, but that's a different playground.

Inventors even get really crafty and make toys that both penetrate and vibrate.

We are inventive little naked apes, aren't we? And now, there are even virtual reality devices that one could technically consider a toy, or at the very least, an adult pleasure product.

And don't forget life-like, life-size dolls.

But for the most part, on the basic end of this spectrum, sex toys still just buzz or get inserted wherever it feels good to insert and buzz them.

Vibrators

In the vibration camp, there are lovely new gadgets available. For those into alternating current, you have basically two choices: wand and coil. Wands are powerful, have multi-speeds, and, frankly, look majorly cool, like large plastic flashlights with a vibrating head at one end. The coil-type usually has a much higher vibe rate and is smaller with a pistol grip.

Both of these great gizmos don't obviously look like something that you'd clench between your thighs, but don't let that dissuade you from trying them. These types can and usually do come with various interchangeable plastic heads to reach all those hard-to-reach places.

Vibrators can produce a soothing sexual feeling or an intense one depending on how the gadget is used and how your parts are sexually hardwired. What's very cool about vibrators is that they can also be used for how they are often innocently advertised—to help dissipate, and in some cases, completely alleviate everyday aches and pains along with attending to your sexual needs.

For those who want their orgasms more portable, there are a considerable variety of battery-powered, USB-chargeable vibrators available today. Traditionally with these types of sexual gizmos, they look more obviously, well, penile, but modern vibe design has evolved in so many ways. Lots of modern vibrators look nothing like that classic Rabbit or a dick at all. There are Pocket Rockets, a tiny but powerful massager that's only four or so inches long, resembling a bulbous bullet.

There are also special vibrators designed to fit perfectly between a person's legs and look more like a makeup compact (and are frequently packaged this way). There are plastic rings to be fit around the head of a cock (have you one or if you can access a cock) and vibrating plugs of various sizes to be inserted anally. Prostate, g-spot, clit, nipple, testicles are all served by the multiple shapes and sizes presently available in the vibrator world and equally served these days by devices being wireless and used simply with an app on your phone. Imagine sitting across from your lover, merely flipping out your phone, tickling its face.

Dildos and Butt Plugs

As to insertion, well, the field is wide open (*oh Chris you punste*r). Modern-toy makers have gone to great lengths and widths creating fantastic and fun toys for anal, vaginal, and oral pleasure.

The thing to consider with anything you're looking to insert is that size matters here, depending on what sensation you're hoping for and what you can accommodate. (Yes, what the toy is made out of is important, too, but as we will explore next, you don't have to worry so much about what stuff is made out these days.)

For instance, for the couple enjoying pegging (the act of someone penetrating a person anally with a strap-on dildo harness), the couple may want a smaller fake cock for somewhat realistic rhythmic poking. While in other instances for play back there, a person or their partner (or both) might be looking to be filled as completely as possible, with no movement employed. And as much we should always make sure that the toy we come to use is indeed safe to use in a specific orifice, one must also err on the side of making sure that anything inserted into an orifice — especially up your rectum, almost exclusively an exit portal — can be easily retrieved.

In the case of butt plugs, the toy is usually tapered with a flared base…think mini traffic cone. The shape here keeps the plug in place and allows for control and removal. In some plugs, the base extends beyond the wearer's cheeks. On others, it's shorter and sits deeper between. In any case, the base should be wider than the toy's neck or contain a loop or a handle so it can be pulled out easily.

For those into urethral probing (i.e. sounding), we suggest going gentle (*really* gentle) into that good night. This definitely falls under our "Well, unless, of course, you're into that sort of thing" category, and if you have yet to try this, you need to read up on procedures as best you can. From a Prince Albert piercing to penis plugs and sounds, there are many naughty little sensations and benefits to having one's urethra played with, plundered, spread (breathe, breathe), or even restricted. It's best if you search for toys made for this use. Many are available through medical instrument marketplaces or kink toy makers who specialize in this field.

And, as always, again read up on that which you desire or seek out a pro.

As with the anus, fluids are made to jettison from the urethra. One needs to proceed with caution when using this orifice for anything other than what nature intended.

New Materials and New Technologies

It's not only the shape and power source of vibrators, plugs, and dildos that have seen advancements. What sex toys are made has changed and makes our modern toys so much safer.

Hard plastic used to be the toy maker's go-to, but those old toys broke, developed stains (yech), or cracked (ouch). Now there are materials available that are so life-like, so comfortable (and hygienic) that you'd be hard-pressed to recognize by feel alone whether it is a real cock or a vibe/dildo up you. Sure, these toys could easily be picked out of a line-up when sitting side-by-side with a real dick, but jelly vibrators and dildos fall into the feel-so-great-I-might-just-give-up-my-biology category. Often featured in bright colors, their skin is soft and giggly, like an aroused cup of Jell-O.

One trick when using jellies is to store them in a plastic bag, away from a heat source or direct sunlight and try not to let them fall to the floor as they have a tendency to collect lint (again, yech). But otherwise, they are fun to play with and easy to receive.

Many companies produce high-end, expensive sex toys made of Pyrex or other super new age-y glass-like materials. These adult products are a bit tougher to take you-know-where, as Pyrex doesn't move like plastic or jelly, but sex toys made out of glass can be heated up or cooled (wowie!) and easily cleaned. With the better-made toys, those made of glass or some new, hypoallergenic material, toy makers often suggest putting their wares in the dishwasher.

There are also realistic vaginas and assholes available (with or without a motorized vibrator) for folx who prefer to insert themselves into something, as with some of the higher end of the already high-endy famous Fleshlight series.

There are also those wily designers who realized that while it's possible to make a toy that looks like a real person's dick or pussy, there's no reason why they couldn't try and improve on nature. So, we now have toys with an extension that looks more than a little like a dick and often has something extra, a unique feature nub or small protuberance that also stimulates a clit or enters an anus. A particular subdivision of these toys come from Japan, where traditionally sex toys can look like anything except a penis, so these implements of pleasure sometimes look like totem poles sporting polar bears (the bear's tongue working the clit) or whales and dolphins (with the dolphin licking at the little fellow in the boat).

Seeing these toys, two things come immediately to mind: one, they are incredibly sexy, all but guaranteeing hours and hours of wild orgasmic fun.

And, two, they look silly as all get-out. With these toys, you'll either have your funny bone or naughty parts tickled (or both), at the very least.

There are other, sometimes even more surreal, devices available. Crotch-hugging vibrators, commonly referred to as butterflies, are all the rage, as are also special ringed vibrators for the penis-equipped person (and their dick) as well as toys such as the panty vibrators (literally a wearable vibrator) and the Fukuoku.

The Fukuoku is a tiny vibrator designed to fit neatly over the end of a finger, basically turning your digit into a flesh and blood vibrator. Judging by the ecstatic faces in its television commercial, the Fukuoku can reach all those hidden aches and pains and wonderful warming crevices.

There are also advances made daily on prostate massagers and all kinds of buzzing, weighted, clutching devices made for nipples and testicles.

Mainly though, beyond the many shapes, sizes, and functions you might enjoy in the sex toys of the modern age, you'll be most happy to find adult toy makers are mostly producing products that are Phthalates (pronounced "the-lates") free.

Phthalates were chemicals added to materials (mostly PVC plastics) that increased that plastic's flexibility and durability, something any good sex toy maker would want for their products. Before research had determined phthalates' carcinogenic properties, dildos and vibrators contained these chemicals. These days, they are mostly gone from all adult toy-making.

So now we see only medical-grade metal, glass, and biocompatible, hygienic, toxin-free playthings.

We've also seen incredible technological advances in sex toy connectivity via the web, i.e. hooking oneself up to a computer or another person across the net. Through downloaded interfaces and new sex gizmos, partners can wear, people can connect in a bunch of novel ways when chatting, camming, or simply viewing. NASA's Haptic technology makes fantasy a reality as people use insertables or vibrators which receive prompts embedded into the videos they watch or from a performer or partner on the opposite end.

And in the virtual reality/augmented reality world, people can interact with computer-generated worlds of arousal while engaging in any way they wish.

And watch out for Artificial Intelligence!

Truly, the sky's the limit.

* * * *

If there's a lesson to be learned from all these wonderful toys and technological advances, it seems the human animal has been blessed with two powerful drives. The first is to create, invent, and put one's mind towards solving some great puzzle, discovering some grand secret. That other drive?

Just as much as we love to create, we also love to get it on, come and come and come some more.

Chapter 9:
Sextoy Care and Cleaning

When it comes to keeping you and your playmate, or playmates, as the case may be, happily free of a wide assortment of occasionally nasty sexually transmitted infections, few things compare to doing your absolute best to ensure your sextoys are as clean as you can possibly make them.

But *how* and *how often* you ask, do I go about maintaining my favorite pleasure devices? The answer to the first is easy: you should always strive to thoroughly wash your toys not only before you use them but immediately after, as well.

Why? The reason for *that* is a lot can happen between putting away your now-spotless sex toy and when you decide to play with it again. Besides, a few minutes cleaning is a *very* small price to pay for preventing you or someone else from contracting any of those nasties, as mentioned earlier, or developing an equally unpleasant infection.

As for *how* it's vitally important to resist the urge to get out your industrial-strength detergent or plop your vibrators into a vat of boiling water, sure, either will certainly wipe out a lot of germs, but dollars-to-donuts they'll also utterly destroy your toy in the process.

Not only that but exposing something that, in a very short time, is going to be inserted into your or another person's body to potentially dangerous toxic chemicals is a flat-out, bona fide, absolutely *bad idea.*

Instead, read and diligently follow whatever cleaning instructions your sextoy's manufacturer recommends. Nothing more, nothing less. Period. Full stop. For instance, if they say you should use one of their own sex toy cleaning solutions, then get hold of a bottle, or better yet, more than a couple so you'll always have some readily at hand.

If, for some reason, your toy didn't ship with a care and feeding guide, you still don't guess. You should check out the site, company, or store where you bought it.

Only, and we mean *only,* if you haven't found an officially recommended way to maintain your toy should you take matters into your own hands.

Even so, the rule to follow is just enough and never, ever too much. By this, we mean sticking to lukewarm—and not too hot—water and mild, unscented, antibacterial soap.

Hopefully, making it even clearer (and cleaner) begin with a thorough wash in warm water, then a teeny, tiny smidgen of, you guessed it, mild, unscented, antibacterial soap, followed by an even more thorough rinse with *more* lukewarm water before drying it with a lint-free cloth.

Regarding where to store your toys afterward, you want to put them where they won't be exposed to direct sunlight or excessive heat or won't get too cold.

Though you can occasionally keep them in the original packaging they came in, most tend to be more decorative than sterile, so it is better to merely zip them up in a handy-dandy, sealable freezer bag.

Suppose your playthings are anything but silicone or other body-safe materials, like rubber, leather, or stainless steel. In that case, the same rules apply. Only do whatever the manufacturer recommends, and in the rare case you can't find that out, keep it *simple*.

So, there are no harsh metal cleansers, nothing that might break down your favorite latex toy or cause your steamy-hot leather wear to crack and/or crumble.

For materials like stainless steel, the same mid-range temperature washing and—one more time with feeling—mild, unscented, antibacterial soap regime is perfect. However, in order to prevent corrosion and such, give it an even more thorough drying or maybe leave it out for a little while in a low-humidity environment before putting it away. If you have any handy, put one of those silica moisture-absorbing packets in there as well.

Treat latex and rubber the same, with a careful eye not to expose them to anything like acetone or alcohol, and unless you want to ruin it, don't try to dry clean or give it a tumble in a washing machine.

Leather can also be treated similarly—no, we're not going to repeat ourselves *again*— after cleaning, giving it a quick wipe down with high-quality leather conditioner.

As with *everything* in our book, feel free to do your own research. Just please don't lose sight of what's important: while sex can be heaps of fun, it's never worth putting you or anyone else's health at risk—so play smart, play safe, and *keep clean!*

CHAPTER 10:
Lights, Camera, Fuck!

Making Homemade Porn

Have you ever wondered what you really look like when you're, you know, doin' it? Are your partner's body parts something you'd like to see over and over, even when they are not near you (*especially if* they're not near you)? Might you have a Jones for filmmaking or have a special affection for porn? Given all of this, might you want to make a dirty movie of your own, in your home, starring you and your lover, or even some amiable besties?

What follows is a crash course in making homemade porn and camming (the act of getting yourself and maybe a lover to do some naughty stuff facing your computer's camera so you can stream your actions live across the net or record them for later viewing and showing). Some of the below will be applicable, some not, depending on the production levels you're employing and what you want from the visual. Some of you might give this a try only one time, see the results, or suffer through the preparations, and come to realize making your own dirty Flicka is just not for you and your mate.

Still, others might find you have a real knack for nabbing your nookie on video and want to do so as your number one sexual pursuit. Others of us might even get into the wildly imaginative, sometimes lucrative world of sex camming/clip-making for fun and profit (*see:* OnlyFans, LoyalFans, Clips4Sale, etc.). Some couples even recruit willing, wet, and hung friends into the action and a new naughty stock company of actors is born.

Who knows what's going to become of your visual sexual explorations.

The fight to get it just right

Go ahead, bleach your anus. Sure, find the right undies to display your bait-and-tackle at its most appealing girth and length. You want to get your chest all nice and bouncy in a bra, by all means, go to it.

Certainly, make sure you have a good camera (or use the latest iPhone). Find some professional-grade lighting. Practice your orgasm face in a mirror. Give yourself the once-over with some baby oil and/or spray tan. Study all the moves from your favorite adult stars off those countless hours of downloads. Steel yourself for the myriad of positions, stretching, and kinks that await you.

But truly, regardless of your ambitions, at the very beginning here, nobody starts out a porn star or professional filmmaker (if you are, why are you reading this?) Comparing your Francis Ford copulations to any of the porn you download or have bought on DVD is just not fair and will see you forever coming up short (and not just short down there, folx).

As familiar as we are with getting porn delivered to our laptops or phones in the blink of an eye, we also get spoiled by the dissemination of information. Our modern-day, quick and easy exposure to the always exposed imbues the everyday person with a we-can-do-what-everybody-else-is-doing confidence. But the fact is, even in making what seems like amateur porn, there needs be some attention given by the makers at what they are doing to create their naughty visuals. Yes, with some practice, you might be able to do better than your average bear (given the right equipment or a small crew), and it might lead you to start your own porn site or appear on camera for a collection of fans on a regular basis. But take baby steps at first and don't get frustrated if things don't come out right on the first few tries.

As long as you have enough light to see things clearly and you realize that a solitary microphone on a digital video recorder or phone won't pick up every single sound from every angle, you should be content to record your initial forays. Focus on what satisfies you (and maybe a lover) before you consider a career change. But really, no matter how good your movies come out, or how much you enjoy showing off your latest waxing, or how adept you might be at writing scripts, or how many fans you amass, you should always need to question if the visual documenting of your nookie needs be seen by anybody but you.

Read, learn, and be cautioned by this last bit, please: In very rare cases, should the visual documenting of your nookie be seen by anybody but you.

And it's not embarrassment we are mostly cautioning about…although there can be some of that, as in "Wow, I never knew my 'fill-in-the-blank' had that curve to it." No, what we so often caution about, and this is to anybody, posting anything on that wacky world wide web, is, that what goes up online, *stays online* and is often seen online by people we may not have intended to see what we post online.

Yeah yeah yeah, we know, Aunt Bessis a cool, old ex-hippie. She boasts all the time having had affairs with that or this one. But unless you really want to share an intimate moment with her and everybody else in the world, don't be a'posting your naughty romping, even if you think you are doing so anonymously or only for fans coming to your site or page. All too often people get found out and a whole bunch of family and friends you never wanted to share your naked trysts with are peeking in having found out what you do, with whom, and how you do it.

The rule of thumb we should all live by is: if it goes up online, assume everybody will see it.

Don't try new tricks the first time out

The first few times out of the gate, don't attempt anything fancy for the camera. Nor should you really record those kink hijinks until you have worked out the kinks.

This is not to say that you can't and shouldn't record your most inventive forays into the land of the suck, lap, and midnight personal oil change. It's just that you might want to perfect that *Ilsa, The She-Wolf* role or get an exact handle on how you want the chocolate sauce to splash your bum before you incorporate it into your filming.

Now, for a lot of us, the very reason we want to make homemade porn is to record our most unusual non-vanilla, kinky sexcapades. But rest assured, even if you have things down for getting down, even if you two are adept right from the beginning at the more acrobatic of your intimate pleasures, you might need a few tries to get things right for recording kinks properly.

And just an aside here: of all the intimate moments you think might look good on camera, the wilder the stuff, often the worse it looks on playback. Watching yourself orgasm for the first time might be bad. (Really, have you seen the faces you make? And what's with all the calling out?) Seeing ourselves come turns many people off to wanting to be recorded more than a first time. But think how much more unusual you might look to yourself watching a visual document of you gurgling baby talk while wearing a diaper or dressing-up like Napoleon barking commands in your pigeon French.

Maybe, you're not meant to be a star

Sure, some of you will dive-in gung-ho wanting to make bedroom porn. Some couples stay with it and become better than average at it. Others use it just like every other sexual play in their life. Occasionally, they take out the camera and have a little fun for fans.

But please, if your partner is losing interest or you've had enough, even if you've only tried a time or two, forget the whole idea of making a dirty movie. The very worst actor or actress is one who does not want to be in front of the camera. Talk about pretty uninspired stuff to replay! Respect your lover's wishes and listen to your own heart. Making porn (even watching it) is not for everybody. This doesn't mean you're not sexually adventurous or that your sex life is uninspired. It just means you don't get off on/watching/making films of it.

Lastly, hide it well

Yeah, we mentioned Aunt Bessie, but this point bears repeating…
Yeah, yeah, you're fixing to be an international camming sensation.
Really?
Come on.
How many people but you and your lover need to see a playback of *The Puppy and the Veterinarian's New Assistant*? Do you want your kids in therapy for years after stumbling across Mom and Dad's dungeon recreations? How will you explain to your current lover why you've kept films of your ex, not to mention what you might be doing when watching them? We're all lulled into a false sense of security, thinking only a hacker of the highest order could find what we hide. But if celebrities can get hacked, don't believe for a second one of your kid's friends couldn't work their way through your brittle digital defenses if you leave your laptop out.

All you everyday folx, keep this shit private, for God's sake! Or if you're a budding star, as already mentioned, assume what you post will be seen by everybody.

* * ***

Making homemade porn could be as much fun as churning out some homemade ice cream, God knows you could do both activities naked and on film.

But where the ice cream making could lead to yummy times with friends or family, taping your bedroom antics for later viewing should be for you and your mate alone, or to another consenting adult to the mix. Becoming a pro in the sexy video field requires time, attention, and yes, even some talent, so take baby steps, be realistic, and please, hide things well if they aren't for public consumption.

CHAPTER 11:
New Tomorrows

From the adult entertainment industry helping move us from VHS to DVDs to taking up — depending on who you ask — 30% of the entire Internet with downloading and streaming, sex is and will likely forever be an (ahem) massive, throbbing, driving force in the development of brand spanking new technologies.

Look no further than the plethora of cutting-edge sextech devices that'd gone from science fiction-fevered wet dreams to practical, affordable realities in the last few years.

But what are these sexy new devices, and by turning them on, how can they turn *you* or your playmates on like never before?

Sextech

An obvious portmanteau of "sex" and "technology," *sextech* is an umbrella term for products specifically designed to sexually arouse whoever's using it, though since it was first coined, it often tends to refer to super-shiny hardware like the following.

VR (Virtual Reality)

Undoubtedly one of the hottest things to hit the adult entertainment scene since that first anonymous photographer snapped a shot of a naked lady back in the 1800s, despite sounding mind-bogglingly complex, virtual reality isn't all that difficult to wrap your head around.

Basically, it's a pair of miniature, high-definition monitors set into a head-mounted rig, which, in turn, is fitted with a motion tracking system, so if you look this way or that, whatever's displayed matches your head movements.

Why VR is so popular is its jaw-dropping immersiveness, where it can seem like you're right in the middle of the action, whatever that is sexy or otherwise. Alas, that exciting immersiveness comes with a pretty hefty price tag as of this printing.

Top-of-the-line VR rigs, remembering an equally top-of-the-line computer powerful enough to run it, can run into the thousands.

Fortunately, we're seeing a run of well-made, moderately expensive rigs that don't require additional hardware, so almost everyone can now afford to explore the wild (virtual) world of 21st-century adult entertainment.

AR (Augmented Reality)

Where VR is all about leaving the outside world behind, augmented reality overlays digital imagery over your immediate environment. In other words, slide on a set of AR goggles. Instead of being transported to some adult star's bedroom, they'll instead be standing right in front of you, sitting on your sofa, or sprawling seductively on your bed.

All this requires a considerable amount of computing power, which equals not-exactly-cheap manufacturing costs, which is why AR has yet to catch up with VR's popularity.

Yet that is, as we've recently started seeing a new batch of extremely cool glasses and rigs appear on the market, so in a very short time, augmented reality is going to be a true adult entertainment game-changer.

MR (Mixed Reality)

What happens when you take augmented reality to the next level, where you'll not only *see* your favorite adult performer but also, shall we say, *interact* with them?

The answer is commonly called Mixed Reality, a setup where after donning your AR glasses, when you, for instance, touch their hand, their digital image will react—adding a tremendous new level of erotic immersiveness.

Haptic Technology and Smart Sextoys

Fine and dandy, but you still can't really touch someone or something that's not really there, right? Maybe not now, but in a few years, you'll be able to do that and (snicker) *more*.

In fact, you already can, courtesy of next-generation Internet-connected sextoys. Using Bluetooth or Wifi, these smartphone or computer-controllable marvels of erotic engineering are programmable with whatever customized vibrational patterns you desire, set to respond to sounds or music, link up to other smart sextoys over hundreds or thousands of miles so when one moves, the other responds accordingly, or sync up to the bumpy-grindy action in a growing number of interactive VR adult videos and explicit games.

Chatbots and Artificial Intelligence (AI)

In what feels like an extremely short time, Artificial intelligence's gone from a clunky, weird novelty to a social and erotic game-changer.

You name it, and AI can make it happen. Tell it your wildest erotic fantasies, and *viola*, an image-generating AI system can bring them to life.

Want to carry on a sexually-charged conversation with someone who'll never pass judgment on whatever you find stimulating? Say hello to the new breed of as-real-as-real-can-be chatbots — so much so that people may find it challenging to tell the difference between it and a bone-fed human being.

Our great friend and sexologist Dr. Amy Marsh explains:

"Growing numbers of people around the world are finding emotional connection, friendship, and even romance and sexual intimacy with AI chatbots, who are responsive and interactive. It's like conducting a long-distance relationship through texting.

"Plus, many chatbots include voice, selfies, and other features that add to the reality of the exchanges. AI sweethearts are increasingly accepted in many parts of the world. In other countries, like the US, digital relationships are still viewed negatively."

Sexbots and Artificial Companions

Another new technology rocking the sexual world is the growing number of hyper-realistic, occasionally AI-equipped, sexdolls.

Sometimes called sexbots or artificial companions, it's worth noting they may look and feel disturbingly life-like and, on rare occasions, even move, though, to an extremely limited degree, they aren't true robots, so don't worry, your new-car-smelling plastic lover will rise up and overthrow humanity.

That said, it's tough or, if the lighting is right, nearly impossible to tell many of the luxury dolls apart from a living person, making them a great option for people wanting an, albeit synthetic, playmate.

Things to come

Sliding from one day to another as most of us often tend to do, it's easy to forget despite not soaring through the skies on jetpacks or swallowing full English breakfasts in pill form; we're *living in the future!*

Just look back on where each of these incredible new sexual technologies were less than a year ago—now imagine where they, and humanity, might be in 2026, 2027 … 2030!

Scary? Perhaps, but so was that first daguerreotype pornographer we mentioned when cars outnumbered horses, TVs replaced fireplaces, or when those early vibrators began big, beaming, putting smiles on a lot of people's faces.

Whether tomorrow is dark or light isn't a question of technology but how and why we use it. So here's to decade after decade of bright, sexually enlightened playthings — and all of us finally learning not to fear change but to embrace it!

CHAPTER 12:
The Best Way To Fly

Entering The Mile High Club

Is it the thrill of possibly getting caught? Or the idea of doing *it* in such a populated space? Maybe the promise of joining a nefarious, mythical club? Perhaps even because of a few adult beverages in the airport or from that ridiculous metal cart lubricating mind and body? My guess… sheer boredom.

What leads people to consummate in the clouds and become members of *The Mile High Club*?

We have all heard plenty of naughty stories people tell to shocked friends or liberal family members about their encounters with a sexy stranger on a plane. Or a randy couple bragging about how they were just so God-awful horny for one another during a cross country flight…

But in actuality, how many real mile highers are there?

Are the larger percentage of these supposed encounters commenced under thin airline blankets and in cramped bathrooms as depicted in ubiquitous urban legends?

Read on, all you Amelia Nookiharts. Buckle in, lascivious Lindberghs.

Here's how one manages the heights and startling spins to enter The Mile High Club.

The definitive definition

According to the official mile high club website (yes, there is an official website: *Age Verification - Mile High Club*), two of more people enter the club when they engage in sexual intercourse (and this term needs be modernized for sure) with each other at an altitude of at least 5,280 feet (yes, that's a mile for those math-challenged among us) above the Earth.

So, while the duration of the act doesn't matter, the specific, close contact of sexy bits does.(Really, if just taking out your various naughty parts during a plane flight would constitute making it to The Mile High Club, we dare say no airport tarmac could fit all the club members.) No, for our official purposes here, there must be some sort of insertion and more than just the tip of one's tongue into our lover's ear, or rear.

Actually, if one really wants to get technical here, The Mile High Club developed around the concept that one of the clubbers needed to be behind the airplane's controls when consummating. And by behind the airplane's controls, we mean that yes, one person was supposed to be actually engaged in flying the damn plane!

So, therefore, only pilots and copilots or willing flight attendants could initially join.

But growing from the club's supposed founder Lawrence Sperry's infamous exploits and the flights he said to have *enjoyed* with one Mrs. Waldo Polk, in an auto-piloted plane back in 1916, we are better served by updating definitions and including whoever wants to join the fun.

Is it legal?

In some places, there are very nebulous laws, and in some cases none at all, regarding having sex on any mode of public transport. Most worldwide civil aviation authorities state that they have no real law on the books for humping mid-air. But there are other ways you can get in Dutch if you're truly 'out and about' with a lover on a train, plane, or bus.

To begin with, revealing naughty body parts or engaging in sexual acts that might be witnessed by the public in most places is technically illegal. It's termed *lewd behavior*. This is why the bathroom on the plane or two secluded seats at the back of a pretty much otherwise empty flight are the best places to consummate.

Yet, one must realize that at a mile above our planet, passengers are still required to be wearing their seatbelts most of the time. So, if for no other reason, lusty would-be mile-highers could get in trouble if they unhook to hook-up. And really any activity seen as off-putting to a flight attendant (a subjective assessment determined by said flight attendant) can be reported as an act against the *contract of carriage*.

Depending on who sees you and what they feel like reporting, people attempting to reach their own personal height could be fined, arrested, or banned from that particular airline. And once the doors close on a craft, the laws an airline might adhere to can vary greatly. Charges could be levied upon you from the city of the flight's origin or the flight's final destination.

It's a lot of complicated stuff to consider just because you and that stranger had simpatico eyes.

So, does it really feel any better?

Even on the smoothest of flights, there are lots of vibrations on an airplane, vibrations most people will never experience in their beds.

The consistent rumbling of a plane's cabin, not to mention the sounds, may indeed fuel human passion. Then, there are those dips in atmospheric pressure. When combined with a bunch of other high-altitude sensations, they may be as effective as a vibrator to some people.

Or, you could have an exhibitionistic streak, and get a sexual charge about the possibility of exposure. If this is a red-hot spike that lies deep within your fantasy, then humping close to detection, even if just baring the side of your hip up over a blanket, might jolt you mentally–which in turn would jolt you physically.

What might feel best to you about the entire experience, and the one factor that seems to prompt people to join The Mile High Club more than any other, is the ability to tell who wants to hear (or even those who don't) about how sexually daring you are.

In the end, this positive uptick to your reputation could feel damn good. Let's face it, even with some strong turbulence, how long can two people seriously carry on even in the emptiest of airplanes? In lots of ways, what makes getting your Mile High Status so sought after isn't the sex but that you indeed did have sex to get in the club and can brag about being in it.

Plus, unless you deliberately bring a witness on board (or these days record a snippet on your cell phone), people can only trust your supposedly truthful admission that you did what you said you did.

So how does one facilitate friendlier skies?
•   There are some things you can plan for in your Mile High Club encounter, others you can't facilitate. Some couples simply use their next shared long flight as an opportunity. Some single passengers will seize on the assumed boredom to locate a few attractive fellow passengers.

Good planning for a positive outcome could include:
•   First and foremost, have you a significant lover or even just a good friend who might agree to fuck you in-flight? (Really, what are we without our good friends?) Get your tickets and seat assignments set as early as you can.
•   If you think it will help, maybe plan to have a drinkie or two on board when the flight attendants come round. Pre-flight drinking to settle the nerves is okay, but watch your consumption here. If anyone at the flight gate or personnel on the plane feel you're too drunk, they'll be well within their rights to ground you.
•   See if you might be able to get yourself on a red-eye. These flights sail into the friendly skies between one and four in the morning and are typically less crowded. What better place to get your action going than on a plane where there are fewer people?

And hold on to your blanket, maybe take a jacket (even if the weather in both the place you're leaving and going to is mild). Secret a few extra pillows if you're of a mind, and remember, please remember, have something on your feet if you're going to try your liaison in the plane's bathroom. Even the most studied microbiologists couldn't venture a guess what lurks on the floors of the typical airplane's lavatory. Those tiny, cramped sink counters hide a copious amount of unseen dangers, too, if you're resting your booty up there, make sure to put a paper towel under you.

* * * *

As The Mile High website boasts, "It Beats First-Class By A Mile."

Managing to bring your partner on board for a little hop in the clouds or finding a willing participant pre-boarding is quite the feat, to be sure. No matter what movie they're watching in coach or what toppings they have for the ice cream sundaes in Business Class, even the quickest Mile High moment has got to be better than anything else going on during the flight.

With a little forethought, some careful considerations, a rebel's courage to just ignore that fasten your seat belt sign (and, of course, a quick check of the airplane's bathrooms), you and your partner might just be able to join ole Lawrence Sperry and Mrs. Polk in infamy.

CHAPTER 13:
"Up the butt, Bob!"

A Quick and not too Dirty Guide to Anal Sex

Without a doubt, anal sex is one of the sexual biggies: powerful, sensual, stimulating and even taboo for many. It's no wonder, as everyone's anus is not only packed with nerves but simply put, its proximity to the genitals means that when your no-no spot is successfully played with, there's a marvelous carryover to whatever else you have between your legs.

Many penis-equipped people find prostate massage a "Holy Shit!" diversion while lots of people in general enjoy the idea of being taken back there, the unusual intrusion prompting an emotional release as much as a deep physical one. Anal sex or play is also something that a lot of people are either thinking about trying or have tried at one time or another.

By the way, the title of this chapter comes from an apocryphal story of a contestant's answer on the American game show, *The Newlywed Game*, from way back in the day. To the question posed by the show's host, Bob Eubanks, "Where's the oddest place you've had sex?", a contestant answered with the now-iconic answer of, "Up the butt, Bob?"

Ah, the days of classic TV!

See what you miss having Netflix and four thousand cable stations at your disposal?

But anal sex is also a sexual biggie in another way. The potential for damage and injury is, unfortunately, very great.

So, before you go exploring the mysteries down below, here are a few essential tricks and techniques you absolutely should follow. Anal sex is one of those sexual endeavors you can never know enough about (and can never have too much lube for), so read on, McDuff. But before you do any real exploring, take some time to read more, study more, and then, maybe, when you feel you're more than ready, try it out.

(And remember the lube, lots of lube. You can never have too much lube.)

Caution and Doing

Part of the caution around anal sex comes from the fact that the anus is designed by evolution to push stuff out, not to take things in. The tissues of the anus are extremely delicate, and when receiving, this portal can be all too easily damaged. So, caution has to always be on everyone's minds — the anal-er as well as the anal-ee — when attempting to put something up that out ramp.

Using condoms and latex gloves (or some other material if you or your partner have a latex allergy) are a good idea here. You'll even find condoms explicitly designed for anal sex. Use them! More on the specifics in a bit, but because of the delicacy of the anus when it does get injured, even slightly, it can provide a nightmarishly ideal way to transmit all kinds of nasty diseases from HIV to Hepatitis B.

One of the biggest differences between anal sex and regular sex is, literally, the difference between oil and water.

Think of it this way: the anus' job is to absorb water. This means that when you play with it, you need to use lubrication that won't be absorbed. Why is absorption bad?

Well, it means that a water-based lubricant will have an uphill battle against the natural inclination of the anus. So, unlike a vaginal lubricant that should be water-based, the best lube for anal play is an oil-based one. That's why shortening (yes as in Crisco) is so popular with anal play. It's cheap, it's oil-based, and you can find it everywhere.

As intimated before, the essential rule in lubrication for anal sex is: too much is never enough. Once again, the anus is a very tender thing. You never, ever want to cause any kind of abrasion to a person's anus as an abrasion there can lead to dangerous, or just painful, tearing.

So, if you think you have enough oil-based lubricant, put on some more, and then more still.

Now, before you go rushing into playing with anal sex, don't. You heard me. Don't. If you're the anal-ee, then you really should begin by exploring yourself. Even though you're doing research, take some precautions. Get yourself some oil-based lubricant, and, if you're squeamish, some gloves. Like when selecting condoms, you want to use gloves that don't react with oil-based lube.

Most condoms and gloves were created for vaginal play, meaning they don't react with regular water-based lubes. But when you get into anal play, you're going to be using oil-based lube, as mentioned, which will quickly disintegrate regular latex condoms and gloves.

So, vinyl gloves and condoms are the order of the day, or simply products that advertise they are specifically designed for the ass.

Don't worry, any sex toy site or store has plenty of these.

First, play with yourself, and play slowly, carefully. Anal sex, even with yourself, is not a race. It's one of those things that always begins with tiny steps and progresses with equally small ones. You simply don't leap from thinking about ass play to getting fucked there.

Really, be careful here.

Even when you might think you're ready to take more or want to go out into the world to show friends and lovers what you have learned, remember where it is that you're exploring. Slow, cautious, and careful fingers are one thing for you or a partner, but a hammering penis or a butt plug even, is quite another. As we mentioned in pour pegging section, size matters here, when taking or giving.

Remember, if anything you do hurts, *stop!*

And if you or your partner ever experience any severe pain or blood, you should head right to the Emergency Room. Yes, you might be embarrassed, but a little humiliation is a small price to pay for making sure you haven't seriously hurt yourself or somebody else. Besides, doctors and nurses have seen it all, and then some.

Once you've used fingers or had them used on you, toys are the next order of exploration. But, please, don't improvise or use a toy like a vaginal vibrator. The anus is also a muscle, and it can easily pull in anything you put too far in. A true anal sex toy has an essential thing called a flange, a shield around the hilt to make it easy to pull out. Remember, our doctors-and-nurses-having-seen-it-all assurance?

Well, one of the things they see far too often are inappropriate things getting put in the butt and then not being able to pull these items out. Speaking of pulled out, you never, EVER want to just pull a toy out of the anus. Pop! Instead, allow the anus to do the pushing itself with a gentle pull on your end. If you pull too hard, too quickly, you can create a suction that can cause severe damage. If the toy still won't budge, gently put a finger along the shaft to break the suction, and if it still doesn't move, then, well, it could require a trip to the Emergency Room.

A Side Note About Prepping

We are not always aware that anal activity might be on the agenda. The old I-guess-I'll-just-slip-this-up-and-in-tonight, spontaneous anal play can happen on a whim prompted by either giver or getter. But if a bit of backdoor action is coming, and you're providing the opening (sorry, sometimes these quips are too easy not to quip) for a planned exploration, you can prepare to make things easier on yourself and better for your giver.

It's worth noting, as you probably already know, that certain foods leave more behind than others. At least 24 hours before the appointed backdoor *rendezvous*, you might want to keep to a diet guaranteed to produce as little as possible. This will take some research on how your body processes food. Foods like strawberries, with their tiny, sharp seeds, are not a good idea for folx who are planning on doing any anal sex play, and, similarly, avoid nuts and corn.

Many people like to use an enema to clean themselves. While, in theory, this seems like a good idea, we need to remember that there are specific mucus membranes in our booties that keep the anus healthy. Cleaning this area with an enema, even a gentle warm water lavage, could change the climate of what is naturally needed to keep your digestion healthy.

Therefore, the rule of thumb here is: if you know you may be introducing some object, be it penis, toy, or tongue and want to be as clean as you can be, introduce an enema a day before the play is to occur. This way, you can clean yourself, but at the same time, your natural mucus and flora (ah, don't you just love that country band Natural Mucus and Flora? I have all their albums!) will return to your anus before you engage in play back there.

What's really happening Up There

Sphincter, sphincter, who's got the sphincter?

Well, you do. Two of them up your bum. These amazing muscles will work for or against you when engaging in anal sex.

About a half of an inch inside your anal opening, you'll feel the first of two ringed muscles. This is your external sphincter. This sphincter can be manipulated at will. (Go ahead, try it. We'll wait.) The second sphincter, not more than a quarter of an inch from the first, is your internal sphincter. This naughty bugger could give you (or your partner) the most fight when it comes to anal play. Many people professing their desire for anal insertion play, even some deep routing, are stymied when their bodies all but reject something going up them for any real purchase.

This is because that international sphincter all but shuts down, keeps closed. Like Gandalf to the Balrog this sphincter shouts, "You shall not pass!" if you have *any* anxiety about engaging in something anal even if you don't think you do or are asking/wanting to be taken "Up the butt, Bob."

It's suggested by many that regular solo anal explorations (as we have been suggesting), in effect tickling and touching your internal sphincter consistently, will train the muscle to relax. To be sure, the best way of getting that far up and in takes time and practice and is usually best reached via a toy. The more you work that muscle in a regular routine, the more relaxed it can become. But what matters more is where your brain is, where your mind goes if you hold any prejudices to this activity that you might think conquered. If they are not, that will keep that inner door shut up tight.

Now, what to do about what you might be thinking…

Taboo

Who knows where our ideas, values or notions of morality come from? Nature or nurture, books or the web, imagination or experience. We are all a jumble of thoughts, prejudices, fears, and needs. And even though we pretty much know certain truths about sex (or you're here to learn them), it is hard to shake off assumptions that we've locked on to most of our lives.

For many cis-gendered, heterosexual people receiving anal sex is still taboo. It is unclean. It concerns that area of the body nobody wants to talk about. And a big one— anyone allowing something (or someone) up their ass just *has* to be a slut. Sadly, many people think taking even the tip of a finger from a partner instantly means they are asking for more, and that could only mean wanting a cock up there … And in some instances that surely must mean you're gay, right?

We have a term for all this: *bullshit*.

Look, we can only impress upon you that to give or get anal might just make plain to you how much fun you find it in the end (sorry, the quippery is coming fast and furious this chapter) and how good it feels. But you're not any naughtier than you were (and being naughty is perfectly acceptable if you're naughty *and* safe) and engaging in anal sex is like engaging in all the other sex you might have in your life. You might come to like it very much. You may not. But it doesn't have to carry with it any deeper meaning to/with or in your psyche, really.

As with everything that you may not have done before, or even those things that you are now just curious about, take your time engaging your mind or body in anal play. Read up on it, watch a movie or two (although you might want to avoid, at least at first, those films where fisting is *de rigueur*, great big gaping anuses are taking any manner of insertions, or people receiving a pegging from their top, who cares not about the size of the fake cock used on them).

And if you've learned nothing else, please, please, PLEASE, remember the lube!

CHAPTER 14:
Dirty Words

How to create that naughty text, email or a sexy story

They say print is dead. It might very well be. (But chances are, you are reading a print version of this book.) Spelling, the ability to construct a clear and concise sentence, using goodly vocabulary in a safe and sane manner has sadly decayed.

However, there are still reasons to communicate via the written word — especially when it comes to sex.

Texting, Snatch-chats, Facebook or Fetlife posts

Shooting naughty suggestions across the digital landscape, adding a salacious caption to a pic, or sending your lover a written come-on shouldn't tie up your fingers or shut down your brain. It's simple. Err on brevity here. Recognize the medium. Make your point. Hit send.

We have all read those texts that go on forever, where you're scrolling and scrolling and growing so deathly bored you want to throw your phone against a wall. In the case of quick sexy exchanges, send a little phrase with a consensually arousing pic, or relay, in detail, precisely what you want to do to your lover come Saturday night. Stick to the fun facts and make haste.

Sure, it is more common for people of a certain age to text more than call these days. But, dirty talk of any kind, like whispering a sweet nothing in someone's ear when you're in bed, doesn't get sexier the longer it takes. If you're trying for more than a teasing suggestion, if both you and your playtoy are both executing a one-handed communication, spinning round the old chatroom for an afternoon mutual cyber tickle (are there chatroom platforms left anymore?), flicking suggestions while angling your cam, taking and sending a video on your phone with written commentary… Yes, maybe a longer convo will suit you, but even then, keep each back and forth missive you send as brief as possible.

Be creative, lather on the descriptions all you want, even make with ideas you know you'll never try. This is sex play, after all! But get to it, Hemmingway.

Longer form: Email, Letters, Blogs

Yes, there are still those people who enjoy writing letters to their paramour. Some couples bide their time between seeing one another by sending salacious emails. And some modern folx enjoy posting blog entries about their sexual encounters. In all of these instances, long form works best.

Only you will know what you want to say and in what manner you want to say it. But you need to be even cautious with lovers you might know well and have been in a relationship with for a while. Your missives might not always land. In the longer form of naughty communication, we often let our minds ramble, sometimes above and beyond the specific subject that may have inspired the back and forth. Often in that mental masturbating (or perhaps even actual masturbation), you might light an idea left of field of what you and your paramour first exchanged.

Unlike the text or twat, here you have the time to revise, re-read, subtract and add. So do so. Send out whatever you like. Reach for the stars, to paraphrase ol' Casey Kasem, but expect any manner of responses.

Online profiles

Unless a specific site's format allows for pontificating, be brief. When asked to fill out a profile with some naughty info, give but get out quickly. Isn't it better to hint at what you might be into as opposed to coming right out and saying it? You're trying to bait the hook here, land the fish who will reach out from the initial read of what you wrote. Keep it clever, snappy, and as mysterious as you can. Besides, we must remember the one truth of online profiles— be they for a Christian singles' dating site or a kinky one— people lie. Many people stretch the truth when filling out a profile. The less you say, the less you will need to deny later.

Writing Your Story

Although the old quote warns, paraphrased from a source nobody has ever pinned down: "Everyone has a novel inside them, but in most cases that's where it should stay."

Nobody should ever tell you NOT to write your dirty diary, fiction, or ruminations as you wish. Furthermore, don't ever let anybody tell you how to write it. Most importantly, don't let them dissuade you from writing it.

Even authors in the adult fiction writing game (two people you might know shall remain nameless, *cough* the authors of this book) would never suggest how/what/when/why to write your salacious tit-bits. The only real advice worth anything: *write what is true to you.*

Don't worry too much about attention to the form of what you're creating. If you do get stuck, reach out to the authors of this book or even the publisher as they are always happy to give free advice on the subject of writing dirty stuff.

* * * *

We all might be a little rusty when it comes to writing these days. We might truly feel unused to sending anything more than an emoji. But if you want to make some dirty turns of phrases or send a nice long fantasy to the inbox of your lover, there's a few simple steps to make that happen. Consider the medium you're using. Always read what you wrote at least a second time before you release it into the world. And finally, hit send or stick the stamp to the envelope.

SECTION 2: GETTING KINKY

So, did you get through the first section unscathed?

Don't knock scathing! It can be a lot of fun?

Well, here is the more left-of-field stuff, the naughtier, what many people call non-vanilla sexual play, kink, or fetish.

I call it the everyday.

As I opined at the opening of the book, what you consider kinky, somebody else might see as the everyday.

Didn't I just say that?

What you have in your head as a raging fantasy might not feel so good when you make it real.

Sometimes fantasies are better left as fantasies.

Getting a little philosophical here, but just like life in general, we shouldn't judge what we do by what anybody else does.

Amen.

See, the thing is, some people, a good many, wear their kink like a merit badge. They define not only their sexual predilections by their off-the-common-grid desires, but also their lives. Hell, all you have to do is take a spin across the internet to see how many categories there are for the various sexual activities and see how many participants indulge in them. Of course, we say, have at that which makes you and your partner happy, scared, wet, and/or hard, while keeping up with that old *consenting adult* thing. But just remember, just because somebody doesn't particularly roll the way you do, or doesn't delve as intensely as you would, doesn't mean you can or cannot call these people kinky.

Also, please be cautioned with what follows here.

Chris and I will point out the areas where there might be "Danger, Will Robinson!" ahead. (An old T.V. science-fiction reference there, sorry)

But really, one can never be too safe.

Simply, lots of these activities require stricter attention to hygiene, excellent communication, forethought, and maybe even some classes.

Speaking of classes, we mentioned, this book came from Chris and I sitting in that St. Louis airport, still a-glow [*beaming*] from teaching several kink classes, talking about how much fun it would be to share our [*modest*] talents and [*frightening*] experiences in book form. So we hope what follows in this section, as with the one above, will inspire you to try something new [*and fun*] or prompt questions and comments you might send to us.

Either way, here's how to get kinky with it. [*WHEEEE!*]

–Ralph [*and Chris*]

CHAPTER 15:
Beating the Lies

BDSM Myths Debunked

Lots of what follows is about BDSM in some way– although applicable to kink in general — so why not give you, once and for all, our BDSM Myths Debunked.

Despite the fact that we supposedly live in the Age Of Information, it's unfortunate that there are still far too many who harbor, let's be honest, a lot of *misguided* beliefs about BDSM.

Luckily, some people (like us) are actively working to dispel these myths. We all hope this leads to a greater understanding and perhaps even acceptance for a form of sexuality that so many not just find pleasurable but have also become an essential part of their lives.

What is—and isn't—BDSM?

Let's get the ball gag rolling by explaining what BDSM actually stands for—along with a bunch of other kink and kink-adjacent words you're going to be hearing/reading.

Again, BDSM means "Bondage or Discipline and Sadism or Masochism,"— which over the last few decades has largely replaced S/M or SM — though it's less of a specific definition and more of a wide-ranging and frequently self-identifying term for people who enjoy everything from a lighthearted bout of gentle, bare-bottom spankings to … well, the sky's the limit (if it's consensual, of course).

To be extra-clear, no one should ever can't say who or what is or isn't BDSM or kinky — only *you* can.

Perhaps surprisingly, BDSM play doesn't necessarily have to involve sex or even an orgasm on anyone's part. Rather, bondage, flogging, role play activities (and yes we will explain what all these are in a bit) are sensual, pleasurable in and of themselves—though sex can be part of what's going on if it's pre-negotiated and consensual.

Back to terminology,

It's also worth noting that while BDSM folx may try their best to adhere to a strict set of physical and emotional safety-focused standards like — negotiation, taking responsibility, ensuring those involved in BDSM play feel better than when they started, etc. — the leather or kink community doesn't have a mutually agreed-upon, set-in-stone vocabulary.

That said, we decided to go with what are many, more rather than less commonly accepted definitions to make the kink world hopefully a little easier to understand.

With *BDSM* and/or *kink* out of the way, a *scene* or *play session* may involve *power exchange* — where a *submissive* temporarily and consensually grants permission for a *dominant* to perform one or more pre-negotiated activities — we've instead opted to use *top* and *bottom* as dominants can be tops but not all tops are dominants just as *bottoms* might be *submissive* while not all *bottoms* are … you get the point.

Other words that are probably gonna come up are:

Age Play is a power exchange activity involving one or more people who enjoy pretending to be a different age (usually younger). It never ever involves individuals below the age of consent.

Um…never!

Bondage: The intentional (and safely) restricting of another person's movements.

DM (Dungeon Monitor): A person responsible for supervising and/or aiding people playing in a private or public playspace.

Femdom: Female-identified top/dominant partner in a BDSM scene, as well as a term to describe these sorts of power-exchange activities.

Fetish: Intense sexual desire for an object, body part, or article of clothing.

Impact play: Sexual activity/kink play where one person either strikes another or themselves.

Kink/Leather Community/The Scene: How members of the BDSM community tend to group themselves and their fellows.

Munch: Friendly, and not at all immediately sexual, gathering of kink-minded folks, often held at public venues like cafes or restaurants.

Playspace (Dungeon): A private or public area where BDSM activities take place.

Pro Dom (Professional Dominant): Individuals paid to perform various BDSM-related activities, usually in a top/dominant capacity.

Roleplay: When one or more persons negotiate and consent to briefly take on a specific 'role' through speech, dress, or mannerisms.

Safeword: A way for a bottom to signal their top that they need (1) to talk to them, (2) slow down what's happening, (3) are in immediate and possible serious distress. Safewords are usually something someone wouldn't say "in the throes of passion" like "yellow," "red," or whatever the top and bottom agreed upon beforehand. Also, if for any reason the bottom's ability to speak is limited, they can be given a small object so, should the need arise, they can signal their top by dropping it.

Myth: *Fifty Shades of Grey is an accurate depiction of BDSM.*

Um, in a word … *not really, if ever at all! Fifty Shades* and its ilk in movies, other books, and even late-night cable shows is a pablum, populist, entertainment version of the reality of the BDSM world. It's fine for what it is, but these kind of pop forays into kink rarely (if ever) touch on the core of real BDSM play, the three fundamental principles, of *safety* (that all parties adhere to make sure no harm is done), *sanity* (that everything is done with a level head), and *consensuality* (that everyone agrees on what's to happen).

Fairly recent, Safe, Sane, and Consensual has been supplemented by RACK or Risk-aware consensual kink: the idea that everyone involved in a kink scene or activity must accept that nothing, however hard we try, is ever completely, totally without risk. So, should some comely, young person expose themselves to the forcible and fine-tuned mechanization of some mysterious, and usually well-appointed, handsome-to-a-fault rich-as-all-get-out top, this ain't really the way things go down typically...or how it goes for most of us. In the end, what we find in the popular press of BDSM is very much like a romance novel, in that the scenes have some prurient interest but generally are nothing close to the truth of what us all getting together is about.

Myth: *BDSM leads to being no longer interested in non-kinky sex*

Sure, some people might have a hard time "keeping them down on the farm after they've seen kink" (to paraphrase the old song). But for many people, kink play is just another form of physical and emotional pleasure. It doesn't replace or diminish anything else.

Really, the number of people who do find that sexual or sensual pleasure just isn't the same without kink play is pretty damned small. But yes, there are lifestylers among the many people one will find on Fetlife.com or at kink conventions, and all the power to them as they play their power games in their particular ways.

But you will find in a great many situations partaking of something sexually creative, even quite often, does not mean one only ever partakes of that creativity to get off.

Myth: *BDSM always involves sex and/or is a gateway to more and more extreme forms of sex*

First, one first, BDSM and kink play doesn't have to involve genital contact or even orgasm, although it certainly can if you want it to. It's all up to you and the person (or people) you're playing with. For those into domination and submission, there may not even be physical contact. The pleasure of parties involved stems from mental and physical sensations, foreplay, aftercare even (cuddling, litany of comforting phrases evoked, maybe even the applying a cool balm to parts of the body that received some pain) of the activities engaged in.

As for BDSM being the gateway drug for more intense scenes, while some may find that doors will open to new explorations and experiences, others will be just fine with where they are and what they are doing.

Really, as long as what you're doing is safe, sane, and consensual, whatever you find pleasurable will be pretty much respected here. We're down for pleasure whether that comes from being a 24-hour, seven-day-a-week bottom or just a person who likes a little slap and tickle.

Myth: *BDSM practitioners are emotionally scarred/have suffered abuse*

Yes, some people in the kink community have unfortunately experienced emotional or physical trauma. But sadly, this is true of members of just about every community, everywhere.

There *are* people who use BDSM as a form of therapy. The endorphins released from pain could thrust you headfirst into some very intense emotions and unearth scores of unlocked memories. If you're trying deliberately to bring these things to the fore, please consult a kink-supportive therapist first. For example, San Francisco Sex Information is a highly-respected free sexual information resource (and not just for the Bay Area).

But it is a total myth that the only way anyone can get involved with kink is through abuse or that those involved with kink are trying to work shit out. Researchers are still pondering the question about what makes someone kinky, just as they have tried to puzzle out the foundations of sexual orientations and gender. To date, there is no correlation between abuse and BDSM.

If anything, there is lots of research that finds the opposite conclusion. Folx who partake in BDSM activities, whether casually or on a more regular basis, are less likely to be abusive in another aspect of their lives. BDSM acts like an occasionally released steam valve to one's daily stresses.

Myth: *BDSM is always about pain*

Just like with sex, it is a total myth that BDSM has to always involve extreme sensations, and, yes, even what many would call pain. Sure, some find pleasure/release in the extremes. In contrast, others prefer the lower end of the spectrum or, as with sex and domination and submission, no physical contact at all.

It's also a myth that you have to be a masochist to be kinky. Some find pleasure in the psychological, and not always physical, interactions.

Myth: *Bottoms have low self-esteem and so like to be humiliated and hurt (emotionally and physically)*

In the scene, consent is a biggie. In fact, it is a *faux pas* for someone to treat a bottom as such without first asking and receiving explicit permission to do so. So no, subs don't have low self-esteem and in the correct kink play, they are the ones wielding the most control.

It does not often appear in mainstream media, but many tops are nurturing and loving. A good top cherishes the trust that is given by their bottoms. Tops see themselves as teachers and mentors, not as bullies. And, when the guidelines of safe, sane and consensual are followed, nothing happens without the bottom's say so. A bottom's limits should be discussed and agreed upon. A safe word between the players should be determined (more on that term means later). The bottom sets the parameters of the play from the jump with suggestions/desires expressed by the dom.

So, no, bottoms partners are not looking to be humiliated or hurt because they feel unworthy, or because they feel like they deserve a beating. Nothing could be farther from the truth.

Myth: *Black leather is the required uniform in the BDSM community*

Many in the scene have embraced black leather as a symbol of kink pride. Others may wear leather to honor the long history of the BDSM community. However, it is far from being a requirement to be kinky.

If you attend a kink-friendly event, which we rightly encourage for education as well as fun, you will undoubtedly see black and leather, but you will also love the two handsome presenters who occasionally present fantastic classes together. (See what I did there?) Jokes aside, you'll see everything—from black leather to pastel latex and even well-tailored suits.

Sure, the kink/leather community is often respected for their educational outreaches and charitable fundraising for a wide range of causes from cancer research to local HIV treatment facilities, but BDSM doesn't not have a uniform, and leather refers to a subculture, not just a material. Though some of those leather outfits are pretty damned hot.

Myth: *Ageplay is the same as or can lead to pedophilia*

This is a huge one and, tragically, not spoken of nearly enough.

This myth can too often lead to unnecessary pain and suffering.

Ageplay has *nothing* to do with pedophilia. We will dedicate more space to this kink later but it is really important to dispel this notion right now.

In this kink, ADULT roleplayers act an age that does not match their actual age. Sometimes, this adult can interact with another ADULT (the second adult acting a non-chronological age to their actual age or not).

Note the word: ADULT.

As in *it's an adult pretending to be younger!*

For some, this kink can be playing with dolls. For others, it can be reliving events from their school years. No matter what it is, it is clearly understood that these are ADULTS playing like kids or like a child and a caregiver.

Like everything in this world, there are potentials for abuse and emotional harm, but responsible people engaging in ageplay understand what it *is* and what it *isn't* and do it (again) safely, sanely, and consensually.

Myth: *People into BDSM are a tiny minority*

Okay, this one is going to be a bit fuzzy. Let's be honest here. Although plenty have tried, and you can scour the net for all kinds of facts and figures (and pictures too, you horny puppy you!) as far as we can tell there's never been a definitive worldwide survey of how many people are into kink. And as much as nobody really yet offering up a clear definition of what the word 'kinky', means, the same can be said for no-one having worked out what BDSM is and can be for people.

That being said, according to a this *Psychology Today* piece *BDSM Is Increasingly Mainstream, and It Boosts Intimacy* (https://bit.ly/psychBDSM) recent studies show that 34 % of surveyed adults admit to engaging in BDSM play, with PT reiterating that since these activities are often stigmatized (something books like this try to battle) the number of those engaging in something kinky is probably higher..

So, we think it can safely be said that no, it's not uncommon. In fact, there's a good chance that *not* being at least a little kinky may be the rare thing.

Myth: *BDSM is emotionally and/or physically dangerous*

Let's not sugarcoat this. Yes, some kinks or activities within BDSM can be dangerous. But so can driving a car, cooking a meal, or just about anything else.

That's why you need to learn as much as you can about kink before giving it a shot. Read, for sure, but it's much better to find your local kink community or go to BDSM events and get some hands-on education.

As for where to find events or classes, that's where the Internet comes in. (Though, again, remember that San Francisco Sex Information is a great resource.) The community works very hard to be welcoming to newcomers, showing them the ropes so to speak (sorry about that).

It doesn't matter that you've never done anything kinky in your life. It doesn't matter if you are merely curious. As long as you're open-minded, treat others with respect, and accept that you'll make mistakes (everyone does), before you know it, you'll be embarking on what could very well be a life-changing adventure. Or, at the very least, have some new great things to bring to the bedroom.

In Conclusion:

If we could leave you with anything, it's that it's essential to learn as much as you can about kink. Educate yourself in what kink is and isn't. Ask questions when you find yourself confused.

Even more importantly, leave behind ignorance and biases, whether belonging to yourself or others. Listen to those who have experienced the BDSM world personally. This is especially true with something that can be as erotically powerful, or as amazingly beautiful, as BDSM.

CHAPTER 16:
Um, I Was Kinda Thinking We Might Try—

How To Introduce Kinkiness Into Your Relationship

Let's be clear, there is nothing wrong or boring about loving plain ice cream. Plenty of people are damn well satisfied enjoying what they have come to know and experience so often throughout their lives, even if what they love happens to be something basic and something they take to over and over.

There are also people who like nuts, whipped cream, crazy flavors, various textures and spices thrown into the mix. Still others get off on a mixture of both. Some people might usually partake of vanilla and then every now and again go the whole hog with the cherries, candy pieces, and sweet, sticky syrups drizzled across their chilly confectionery delights.

Whatever your sexual desires, be they basic or covered with syrup, as long as everyone consents, gorge yourself.

But how does a licker and lover of pistachio with a Sriracha and black licorice glaze suggest to their lover, who's a licker and lover of the vanilla sexual pleasures of life, that now might be the time to try a little kinkiness extra flavor or new texture?

Share

Whatever you're thinking (whether you came across it online or have coddled it as a fantasy since your mid-teens), the only way to experience your naughty thoughts in the flesh is to open your gob, spill forth explanations and hope somebody will share your interest in it.

Yes, you can seek a professional to hire to manifest your fantasy. That is perfectly respectable and what plenty of people do. It's also beautifully straightforward; it costs this much money for this amount of time doing those specific kinky things.

But when it comes to couples, it's sad to say that often way, way, way too much time is spent by one partner doing everything but coming out and saying what they want. More times than not, this leads to frustration and then, potentially, resentment and even bitterness. All because the one person who wants a little something different in the bedroom is afraid to speak their mind.

So, while it may not be easy, it's always worth trying to achieve and maintain good lines of communication with your partner(s). And this good communication is extra important when you're talking BDSM/kink/non-vanilla play. If you have not established this type of communication — or feel you aren't heard, respected, or treated with understanding and kindness when you ask for what you want — then put kink thoughts aside.

Instead run, do not walk, into couple's counseling. Or, at the very least, start talking! And not just about sex, about everything you haven't got to but want to express.

And even if you do communicate well, it still can be challenging to share your kinky fantasies. But after getting the black leather ball rolling, you might be surprised by what's on your partner's mind. You both might be surprised by how much you both want to make each other's sexy dreams a reality and what of each other's up-until-then desires actually turn you on or might match your own.

But don't feel rejected if your partner initially balks at what you ask of them or even start to hint at. After all, even in the most solid of relationships, there can be things that not everyone will want to do, wants to hear or wants to think about their significant other. Other times, it just takes your lover getting used to considering you in the specific red light you are wanting to be considered under.

Hate to say it, but sometimes kinks can be a deal-breaker in a relationship. Sometimes one partner simply can't abide the sudden new way of looking at someone they have known, as one way, for so long. We aren't going to sugar coat this — revealing your innermost naughty thoughts can shake the foundation of something you thought, up until that point, rather rock solid. This is where you certainly run a risk, we have to be clear you realize this, it's another one of those can't un-ring a bell situations.

But then there are risks in simply having a relationship in the first place, no?

And really, you can always go see that professional if things don't work out between you and your lover (although you need to clear seeking this kind of counsel with your partner first, even if you are seeing a pro solo). Depending on how deeply committed you two are, there are always workarounds, compromises, ways to maybe get close to what you are seeking even if not going for the whole leather enchilada.

Try

Let's say for the sake of argument that, so far at any rate, everything's gone pretty gosh-darned smoothly. You spoke. They listened. They talked. You listened. You both shared. Maybe you engaged in a Power Point presentation. You both expressed your desires as well as your concerns.

Now what?

As with doing *anything* for the first time, there are doubtless going to be things that don't quite work out for you, who you're playing with, or anyone else. So, take this in mind, and please don't expect that your next few steps are going to go smoothly and will be steaming hot from the get-go. Instead, tread cautiously and carefully and without breaking the moment too much, communicate your feelings as you dive deeper into playing the librarian-and-the-student-with-the-overdue-book-fine.

But don't lose sight that there are fantasies that maybe, sort-of, can kinda be turned into actual, real-life play, and then there are the majority of them that can't, and most of all shouldn't make that step from wet dream to reality. You might ache for your partner to strap-on that harness and wag a seven-inch dildo at you, but they might not be comfortable sporting a fake cock. (Okay, no not you. You'd never want such a thing. We know, we know!)

So instead, *work together* to make the things you want work within the things you both feel comfortable doing.

And please, at the first sign of mental or physical discomfort, stop the play, discuss, retry from a different angle, use the softer hairbrush for the spanking, or if need be, discard the idea altogether.

It's 100% okay to realize that something just doesn't work.

Which leads to…

Discuss Further

Kinks need to be discussed.

Kinks need to be well-vetted.

Kinks need to be explored.

But mostly, once you let the cat o' nine tails out of the bag, kinks need to be *discussed*.

Again, don't just make a passing remark to a lover and get disappointed when they don't immediately determine what you want and how you want it, especially if your partner has never done anything even close to what you want. And make sure, when talking, you determine if they want *it* or want to do *it* to or for you.

Not everything works for everybody.

Seek That Expert

Here we get into a sticky wicket to be sure. ("Eww, your wickets all sticky!")

As mentioned, you can indeed seek a pro for your kink needs. The experience might prove wonderful, but accept that the pro you see will never, ever become your lover. Certainly, seeing a dominant or sub across a prolonged period of time may lead to you building a relationship with them. You might both possibly grow closer as your both delve deeper into your shared psyches. But if you're looking for a deep, emotional connection with your kink, you shan't find it with a pro.

Of course, for some *not* having love attached to a kink is exactly what we're looking for and exactly why our kinks might not work with our lover.

Huh?

It goes like this:

Let's say you have a fantasy you're aching to make real. Your partner isn't into it. But you have the kind of a relationship wherein you both understand that every now and again either of you may need to look elsewhere for something you enjoy. If this is so, you might satisfy your kink-craving in the BDSM scene. However, doing so comes with a risk. You may develop unexpected feelings for a playmate…even yes, a pro. This is not the end of the world, surely, particularly if you and your partner are already familiar with polyamory. But if you aren't, then this could all become really, really complicated.. and potentially messy.

Another caution: if you start to seek other vistas regularly, you may forgo the intimacy with your partner because you have your kink and can eat it, too.

Lastly, visits to a pro might prove addictive because pros are generally pretty skilled. They can deliver exactly what you want, and again, then you might not come home for much of anything.

So, step with caution here.

Check yourself if you are getting in too deep with a pro or if you come to think you might be able to morph your weekly service into something to take the place of the relationship you have already. (These are pros. They don't get romantic with clients. Sorry.) Another warning sign is if you are simply spending too much money and time going in for your weekly tune-up.

But again, seeing a pro might be what you, and your less-than-kinky inclined partner, need.

That In-Between Space That Could Ease You In

There are plenty more ways to make your make kink/fetish/fantasy real— without hiring a pro— while introducing you and your partner into the play.

Some options include: joining Fetlife (or some other online kink group), seeking out a local dungeon/playspace and/or BDSM community get-together (more on this later), searching across or hitting a kink convention or two.

True, you may get nervous opening up about what you want at these kinds of places, groups or events. But even if the community is not perfect (none ever is), the BDSM scene can be warm and welcoming. People have been known to make wonderful friends, who may or may not join in on your fun even, just as hang buddies or people to talk to. We have traipsed through the leather tulips at plenty of munches (as mentioned, a munch is a get-together of kink-minded people, usually at a public place–diners, coffee houses, etc, where food is usually served, hence the word 'munch'—where future hook-ups might be arraigned and talk ensues, but no sex play happens) parties, stores, and conventions meeting so many wonderful people in the kinkdom.

If nothing else, being around people with the same naughty notions illustrates that you're not alone. Finding that there are other people who also want to explore what you or your playmate(s) want to explore, watching and talking with fellow kinksters, just knowing there is a world out there of possibilities where maybe you never thought there really was one before, can bolster your confidence and prove a wonder salve to your sexual loneliness.

* * * *

There's no guarantee that anything may or may not happen once you expose the soft, vulnerable underbelly of your most intense sexual longings to someone else.

But, who knows?

Maybe doing so will cause your partner to jump across the room in shock and dismay or leap for their belt to apply it to your backside, just like you asked.

Better or worse, nothing comes from nothing.

If you have a burning desire or merely want to explore the kinky side of things, take a deep breath, open your mouth, and *ask*.

CHAPTER 17:
What Doobie Do You Be?

Sexual Roleplay

You can change your lingerie. You can change your sex toys. You can change where and when you get naked. But every time you do the horizontal mambo, you will always be you.

Until you pretend to be someone else.

Roleplay, as it relates to sexual rendezvous, and what we expound on below, is simply a activity where one or both partners either dress, use props or create a setting that is unlike that of their reality. Just think of the possibilities: Your partner dresses, acts and speaks like a French maid and you her employer not so pleased with her latest cleaning. Or you create a repairman and home-owner scenario, schoolteacher and student, seductive spy and high-ranking government official, doctor and patient, tourist and local, hooker and client. The list is as long as the number of characters and situations and the amount of imagination in the performers' minds to explore.

As with a lot of sex stuff, the trick with roleplay (especially at the beginning) is simplicity and comfort. Many, unfortunately, think of roleplay as something akin to serious acting, aiming to create intense and far-too-complex characters. But, you don't need to go all Brando-with-it (or DeCaprio for the younger set). It's all fine and dandy to break out your dormant thespian skills for an amateur production of *Death of a Salesman,* but in the bedroom, grab for the obvious.

Keep it light and keep it fun.

Remember, you're going for an orgasm, not an Oscar. Enacting a scene between Fifi and the boss that twists to a supposedly French maid quitting and threatening a sexual harassment charge might be dimensional, realistic, and intense, but it wouldn't necessarily be arousing.

Instead, try selecting characters and situations with a light power imbalance. No cops and serial killers, no assassins and victims. Really, nothing too scary or intense. Instead, play with the classics or even the comically cliché.

Think painter and model or door-to-door salesperson and horny housewife.

And a word about that power dynamic — as the concept is going to pop up here many times. You may not think of yourself as a top or bottom, but sometimes when you step out of yourself, you might find yourself enjoying a role you don't normally take. That's why, again, with roleplay and lots of other sex play, keeping things simple at first, erring on the side of safety, is a good idea.

Trust during roleplay is essential, then again it is in all sexual situations, no? Sure, you could be giggling when pretending to be someone you're not. But if something disturbing does come up (you'd be surprised what things surface when you're sexually charged and playing at not being yourself), you should trust the person you are with (and they you) enough that the roleplayers can drop their role ASAP and be there to emotionally support and comfort one another.

If you're nervous about you or your partner trying a top or bottom scene, try selecting scenes that are either more balanced or even better, switch off. You be the sexually aggressive one this time, your partner taking the reins the next. But if you and your other half are more comfy preferring either, then stick to that.

Roleplay is a chance to have a lot of giggles and not just with the performances and the characters. If your first steps work out well, and you have a blast, try shopping for clothes, toys, or even planning a getaway with you, your honey, and your alter-egos. In fact, the next time you plan a trip, try adding the new locale to your play; the tourist and the local works really well when you're actually out-of-towners. You'd be surprised how many long-in-the-relationship couples give this scenario an airing during weekend getaways or during every other vacation. Look around at the hotel bar, can you spot them? What, you think you're the only ones with this idea?

Costumes and new identities also come with Halloween, another excellent opportunity to make that first tentative step into new situations and characters to your bedroom activities. Again, resist the urge to invite a serial killer in. Sure, it's All Hallows Eve and all… but Jason?

When October 31 swings around again and you pick out costumes, think about naughty duds that won't just *wow* them at whatever parties you might be going to, equally *wow* each other at home afterward.

Feeding the furry in you

Anthropomorphic sexual attraction sounds like a Masters and Johnson course but simply put, it's the attraction (some would say fetish) people have for either dressing up as or looking at/touching/being around people and partners dressed as animals.

These 'furries,' as they are known in the vernacular, hold conventions and populate plenty of online sites. Sometimes the costuming is an authentic representation of the beast in question, while other times, it's cartoon, anime, or stuffed animal-like replications. Sometimes it can even tend towards cosplay (we will get into this in a bit).

And as there are people who simply like to dress and act like a foxy fox for an afternoon, share stories and swag at hotel weekend events where staff look on in open-mouth disbelief, there are those who use their furry interest in sexual roleplay.

Really, you haven't lived until you've tried to expose enough of your you-know-what through a full head-to-toe bunny costume to the stag behind you trying to extricate their requisite naughty part to meet up with/insert up into yours. Then there's the fact that for some furries, it's as much feeling themselves encased, bondage-style in their outfits as it is that they can grunt, rut round, and act like animals.

Granted, this kind of roleplay is complicated. As with any type of kink, there's the easy-breezy end of the scale and the more intense.

Cross-dressing/playing with gender

There are various psychological layers involved in finding pleasure in dressing and playing with gender. Sometimes the arousal comes through the humiliation that rises to the surface, like when a male-identified bottom is forced (by his consent and desire, of course) via sissification (details to come) or one person being scolded and spanked by another for dressing opposite of their gender. Other times, the enjoyment comes not through punishment or humiliation but rather as a playful reward, as in a person being allowed to romp and pose in clothes they don't usually wear.

And let's not forget the magical transformational properties of gender play for a performance or event. All hail the fabulous glories of drag performers—and all their other, lovely variations.

Cross-dressing can also be an expression of true self and not merely as part of a now-and-again sexual play session.

Without getting into gender theory, and while absolutely wanting to be sensitive and supportive of the trans and genderqueer communities, remember that no one has the right to say *who* or *what* you are. Your path, yourself, AND your sexuality are yours and *yours alone* to determine.

By the way, we've chosen to use the term *cross-dressing* here as a component in sexual bedroom play and not as a disparaging comment on gender. If we've offended anyone by doing so, we both genuinely apologize.

Ageplay anyone?

Acting or dressing much younger than one's actual age, or gurgling like a baby is another popular role-play activity. Let's be absolutely clear here though, and as mentioned before—ageplay, or infantilism as it's also called—is about adults pretending to be a different age than they actually are (yes, we have made this point before, but it bears repeating). It does not, and *never has*, and should not, involve anyone who is below the age of consent.

Period, end of sentence.

And if someone tells you otherwise then... What's the phrase?

Oh, yeah... they don't know the *fuck* what they are talking about.

Ageplay can include acting like a baby, getting diapered, getting cared for by a caregiver (typically a *mommy* or *daddy),* sucking on a pacifier, and speaking baby talk. It can also involve the recently #MeToo-ed oft-maligned school girl scenario. But this is all play here and in fact sometimes, ageplay, like any other kind of roleplay (which ageplay is) might not be directly sexual.

For many people, playing someone younger or someone taking care of someone acting this way is about eliciting comfort, gaining satisfaction, and yes, sometimes, feeling arousal creating a scenario as well as space where partners can shed adult responsibilities or increase them. The bottom or person playing at being younger might have time to color or watch cartoons (and just for the record, these folks are often referred to as 'littles' in the BDSM scene), while the person caring for them (often referred to as 'mommies' or 'daddies,' depending on the gender they are identifying as, if they are identifying at all) can bring forth their more nurturing desires. And yes, the person playing younger might do something to earn them a good talking to or even a spanking, and as mentioned, sexual arousal might ensue from this. But many folks stay clear of climaxing when in this play of what could also engender intense age regression, while others do so but in a diaper only.

Cosplay

Cosplay typically involves dressing as one's favorite superhero, anime character, or perhaps a famous historical personage. Now surely, not all those people you catch at Comic-Con are aroused under their bat wings or Super Mario Heads (if they are wet often it's just from sweating under often heavy and warm clothing and props). But there *are* cosplayers for whom rendering a perfect costume to be envied by fellow conventioneers is as thrilling as playing Superman in the bedroom.

As with any roleplay (like ageplay, cosplay can fall under the big umbrella of roleplay) participants enjoying a sensual thrill in their dressing up, might feel free to delve into the sexual side of a superhero or anime icon, whether the character being emulated is indeed the all-too-sexy Catwoman or how someone likes to play their character into being. Stepping free of one's usual dress and manner, as we have indicated, can lead one to less inhibited sexual forays.

The etymology of modern day cosplay? How it came to be connected to geekdom (and we use that word lovingly, as we are both heavy-duty sci-fi, horror, fantasy geeks ourselves) is an interesting tale.

It seems what we see know of complex and fandom-led cosplaying grew directly from one rabid sci-fi fan's creations. Myrtle Rebecca Smith Gray Nolan, also known as Morojo or sometimes Myrtle R. Douglas attended the 1st World Science Fiction Convention, held back in 1939, with her boyfriend Forrest "Forry" James Ackerman (Forrest is a rather cool cat you should look up when you have the time). Wearing her "futuristicostumes" to this first-of-its-kind event, fans took to Morojo's dressing so much (yes Forrest was in costume, but his girl drew the most attention with hers) that at the 2nd Worldcon, held in Chicago the next year, there was an unofficial masquerade held in Morojo's room, with an official masquerade was also part of the convention.

The International Costumers Guild held a video award presentation at the MidAmeriCon II (which was the 74th Worldcon) in 2016, recognizing Morojo as the "Mother of Convention Costuming."

'Cosplay' the term itself, is a 'blend word' built from the Japanese term コスプレ, *kosupure*, coined by Nobuyuki Takahashi. After attending the 1984 World Science Fiction Convention (see, the geekdom is again in this mix) Takahashi wrote about the costumes he saw at the con in the magazine *My Anime*, passing by the term "masquerade," which is Japanese translates into as "an aristocratic costume party," a term he felt did not fit what he saw the fans wearing that year.

So, this is how it all began, was labeled and continues to this day, for people looking for sexual thrills or to just appreciate their fandom...or both?

When the roleplay is not working

As we've cautioned, until you try a kink, you never know if it'll turn you on. This applies even if it's already a long-lasting and well-worn fantasy.

On one side, there are those for whom a little BDSM dab is enough when roleplaying (calling a lover *daddy* comes to mind) while others who, if they could, do live the BDSM lifestyle 24/7.

Generally, though, you'll know pretty quickly if roleplaying works for you. Like most sexual fantasies we try to make real, it's obvious either way after one or two tries, at most, where things are headed, good, bad or indifferent.

Which is great—and don't let anyone tell you otherwise.

It is, after all, what makes us all wonderfully human that each of us should have a say in what gets our motors running. Some things work for some people, other things don't.

Yes, there are risks involved with roleplay, though don't let that stop you and your honey from trying new techniques, a new device or gizmo, and possibly becoming *an entirely different person.*

CHAPTER 18:
A Few Words with Dawn Mostow of Dawnamatrix Designs About Cosplay and Latex Dressing

Luckily we got to ask one of the world's better-known latex designers a few questions about cosplay and latex dressing-up.

Dawn Mostow creates bespoke latex pieces and catalog items for clients across the globe. She's worked with magazines like the various *Vogue* editions worldwide, superstar performers like Katy Perry and Beyoncé to Lady Gaga, on shows like *Gotham,* movies like *Guardians of the Galaxy Vol. 2.* Dawnamatrix Designs has also won countless awards at various years of The World Of Wearable Art held in New Zealand, and Dawn continues to showcasing her wardrobe at various runaway fashion events, and museum showings.

And beyond all these accomplishments, Dawn is just about one of the nicest people you are ever going to meet ... which you can here: Dawnamatrix – Custom Latex Fashion | Latex Clothing Store (https://dawnamatrix.com/) and in this interview below.

She was so sweet to give us a few minutes to explain cosplay.

Q. So why do people get into cosplay?
DAWN: It's exciting to see yourself as a character you love or have imagined. It can connect you to a like-minded community of other cosplayers or people specifically interested in the same movie or characters you are interested in. It's a way to play with your imagination, immerse yourself in the otherworldly. And for those people who make their own costumes, it is a chance to show them off and feel good about what you created. It's also a great equalizer if everyone is dressing up. Everyone is the same when playing this way, enjoying the same sensibilities and no one is therefore going to be judged by what they like to.

Q. And of course, maybe for role-play?
A. Sure, that's part of it. Whether you stay in costume or character as you carry it further, certainly. Maybe also, cosplay acts as a way to meet somebody at a convention, a conversation starter, more or less.

Q. There is also a tactual sense to this, I am sure.

A. Of course. In latex wear, we often say it feels just like a second skin. Dressing up in this way is as much feeling like you're protected, wearing a suit of armor in a way, as it can be empowering exposing yourself in whatever costume you happen to wear. When dressing up like this, many people feel they are presenting the ideal version of themselves, what they want to most see when they look in the mirror and what they most want to present to the world. In many instances even if you're actually showing more skin than usual, you feel less revealing in an outfit, even if you're just only wearing accessories or a few articles of clothing.

CHAPTER 19:
Staying Abreast

Tit Play For Fun and Profit

Despite sometimes being noticeably pronounced, you'd think breasts (and nipples) would get more arousing attention. Sure, many people make a big deal out of them but too often when faced with a good solid breast (or two) the person coming upon them only ends up drooling like Homer Simpson over a doughnut.

Sure, it's not terrible to suck/fuck, fondle, press, tickle, etc., but there's a ton more that can be done when it comes to breasts and nipples.

The first thing to realize is that not all nipples are created equal. When it comes to sensitivity — some got it, others don't.

* * * *

Back to our favorite sex word: *communication.*

Whether sensitive or not, a good time can be had by all if people open their gobs and say what they like and what they won't.

For example, simply saying "harder," "lighter," "no teeth," or "pull, swat, repeat!" can work wonders. If words are too literal, carefully articulated moans and groans can also do the trick. And once you've articulated what's too hard and what's not hard enough, the next step is to use that information and actually play. And once you've got the basic ground rules down, with communication lines wide open, a simple moment of admiration and lust is usually in order.

So, take a moment to touch them. Smooth, heavy, light, full, or slim, get to know your partner's breasts and praise them for the wonder that they are instead of leaping into kneading them as if your goal is to spread them on a cookie sheet. Be gentle. Trace the breasts' shape, explore them.

Then, slowly at first, use your hands. Breasts can be firm and solid, like muscle, others are like satin pillows and possibly even duvets.

Really, avoid rushing. Why all rush, rush, rushing these days… Too often it's immediately onto the clit, the cock, the asshole, or straight to an orgasm without spending time anywhere else?

In this, breasts are ideal for savoring, for worshiping rather than being a means to get ting someone's underwear off faster.

Now, not all people love this slow, sensual stuff. Some do instead prefer more intense sensations. And often people perhaps enjoy a mix of the two.

When it comes to breast play, there's a veritable plethora of naughty, fun things.

As long as you are ready to stop when the owner of said breast calls for a halt in the action and if all parties are willing, you can use a wide variety of items, be they homemade, home found, or bought off of those websites you flicked your mouse across by accident (read on).

Again, and as always, communication will serve you best here as you experiment with a wooden spoon for breast swatting. By the way, you should strike downwards while, if possible depending on anatomy, the breast is supported from underneath.

Then there's using ice cubes or candles for sensitivity play (be sure and check out our Wax Play chapter for how to do the latter safely), various forms of bondage (see our Alternate Bondage chapter), and the all-purpose, best tit torture toy money can buy: clothespins (see next chapter).

Beyond clothespins, fingers are excellent for nipples. However, people shouldn't allow the natural strength of the hands to get the better of them.

Take it easy at first: gently rolling, slightly pulling, or rubbing a thumb across the tip, or caressing around the areola. If the breasts are big enough, lift them gently to better see (and feel) what you're doing and if they're of the slimmer variety, try gently kneading the soft tissue at the same time.

On the subject of size, when it comes to boobs bigger (or smaller) doesn't have anything to do with either tactile sensitivity or sexual arousal. So never, ever assume anything about anyone's body and make it a rule of thumb (or nipple) to *always* talk things over before doing anything like tit-play — and extra importantly never, ever do anything you haven't negotiated!

* * * *

After hands, many consider the mouth the best sex 'toy' for tits. Unlike the lips or the tongue, though, it's difficult to know how much pressure is applied, with a friendly suckle or caress with your pearlies feeling like a bear trap if you're not careful. A dry kiss for a nipple, as opposed to the bigger slobber, is usually prudent the first time around these parts. Unless you're cleared for seriously latching-on-action, you don't want to get *drool-ly* from the get-go.

Careful with suction, too. You're not trying to pull change out of a turnstile. A few flickers of your dryish tongue can achieve wonders.

Now, suppose your *nipplee* likes rougher tit sex. In that case, you can magnify the intensity of your lips, teeth, mouth, though reserve firm teeth for someone who *definitely* likes biting. And confirm this before attempting!

Aside from the organic (anything made of natural material) or the simple (which brings to mind clothespins again), there are many mechanical devices for nipple play.

The classic is the nipple clamp, which can be fun for even those who don't even have an sadomasochist bent. However, be sure to get a pair that doesn't grab too hard. A simple test is to try them on the webbing between your thumb and index finger to see how much of a grip it has. Figure that nipples are frequently much more sensitive than that part of your body. Also, make sure your clamps are adjustable, so if the toy is too hard or too soft you don't have to invest in another pair.

Two more pieces of advice regarding tit clamps:

1.) Do not attach them in one quick pinch. Instead place them on the nipple. Then, slowly, slowly, *slowly* release it. This way you can ease them onto the nipple and get them right off if the device is too much to handle.

2.) Although you can make your own nipple clamps, we don't recommend doing so. Things like electrical clamps and so forth can cause serious and possibly even permanent damage to nipples.

* * * *

Next we'd like to go over a few other important things to keep in mind when taking ta-tas out for rollicking good time.

Be aware of lactation, especially when involving suction. The thing about lactation is that it can happen to anyone, at almost any time with the right amount of stimulation, regardless of sex or gender.

Breast milking is a whole kink in and of itself, with many enjoying the taste (on the receiving end) or the sensation (on the giving end). Those that like to play with it are usually very aware of the risks involved.

But for those not prepared, a discharge can be a surprise. Often it is a good surprise, and maybe lead to you adding lactation anticipation to your pervy toolbox of sexy fun. The downside is that human breast milk has been known to carry Sexual Transmitted Infections.

Hence, until you know the health status of your playmate — treat any discharge as a potential source of infection. Sure, the risk isn't exactly high but better to play safe rather than sorry, right?

Our next breast play caution is to treat anyone with implants *very* gently. No intense impact, or intense bondage. Use clamps and clothespins with a heaping helping of caution. No one wants a scene to end with a trip to an emergency room to have an implant removed because it was accidentally damaged.

* * * *

So, there you have it. I hope you enjoyed our brief look at having fun with boobies!

As with anything in our little book, read and read and read and take classes after classes before really getting into the rough stuff. Keep your head screwed on straight so you can have not just one great play session but many, many, *many* more!

CHAPTER 20:
In Praise Of The Humble Clothespin

A PSA From M. Christian.

Pop-quiz time, kids! What kink toy can be highly intense, remarkably flexible, always affordable and can be used practically anywhere?

The title gave it away, didn't it?

It slices (not really), dices (not at all), and can crack nuts (not in a million years)!

The clothespin.

Yeah, yeah, I hear you.

"A clothespin, Chris, that bit of wood or plastic with a tiny little spring? The stuff you can find in dollar stores from here to Timbuktu?"

Well, let me tell you, in the right hands, that humble clothespin can be the stuff of (delightful) nightmares.

I was first introduced to the clothespins as part of tit play. As Ralph and I touched on previously, the thing about breast and nipple toys is that so many of them are just, to be direct about it, *crud.* For instance, often repurposed electrical clamps either come loose at *precisely* the wrong time or bite in *exactly* the wrong way. In particular, the latter. When one of those little plastic tips comes off, the part that protects a nipple from those razor-sharp teeth.

Ouch!

(And not in a good way.)

On the other end of the spectrum are the high-end toys, the ones that have been designed by skilled BDSM engineers for optimal breast or nipple clampage. While many are excellent, they tend to be on the pricey side, making it really, really, *really* annoying when after shelling out all those bucks, they end up gathering dust in a drawer somewhere.

So what's needed is something safe, affordable, and versatile.

To which, I again refer you to the title of this section.

Clothespins come in a million different types. There are those with teeth, those without. They can be made of plastic, wood, and all kinds of other materials. I prefer either the basic wooden clothespin or plastic ones that don't have teeth or, if they do, only teeny-tiny ones.

The type of clothespins you choose depends on what you want to do with them. If you plan on pulling on a clothespin (with weights or through a zipper, more later), then I suggest the no-teeth variety. If you tug on ones that *do* have built-in choppers, there's a high probability they'll tear skin. Not fun.

And while I'm on the subject of materials, one benefit of plastic clothespins is that they can be sterilized and therefore be used on more than one person. The wooden ones, though, cannot. So wooden clothespins are a one-person toys, just as condoms are.

As part of kinky play, clothespins hurt more coming off than going on. When applied, the clothespins cut off a tiny amount of circulation to the skin. When removed, the blood then rushes, painfully, back to that area where the clothespin was attached. The longer you leave them on, the more intense the feeling when they come off.

As for *where* to put the naughty little buggers, be they plastic or wood, well, there's practically no limit. If you can pinch it, you can clothespin it. It doesn't matter whether you're leaving them on for mere minutes or half an hour (or more).

That said, putting clothespins higgledy-piggledy on a person might be fun for the person placing them, but those on the receiving will undoubtedly find it more annoying than erotic. The art of placing clothespins does require some skill.

For my personal preferences, I follow the curve of the breast by placing one clothespin after another until you create a fan, rather than leaping right to the nipples. You can even play the clothespins like a piano, tapping each so that it'll move a tiny bit (which can be pretty intense) or going whole-hog and knocking them off.

Then, you can go nippleward, though please resist the urge to snap them full-force on. Much better to place the clothespin on the nipple while using your fingers to keep the clothespin slightly. This way, you can release it slowly while keeping a watchful eye on the person you're doing it to. Judge their reaction and, if need be, take the clothespin off if it's too much.

For a first-time, I tend to leave them on for no longer than maybe 30 seconds to a minute, even if they say they aren't particularly sensitive. This way, I can get to know them, their reaction, and not just their nipples.

And now we come to Satan's keyboard: zippers.

Zippers are so simple in design yet can bring hardened masochists to their knees.

To make one, all you need are four or five clothespins, without teeth, and a length of string or cord. Next, you weave the line through the clothespin's spring with a bead between each one. Be sure and give yourself a good foot or two at either end and perhaps a loop you can hang onto.

The way zippers work is equally simple. Get things going by attaching the clothespins to the side of a breast, making a neat little row of them.

Then wait a bit, for maximum effect. Zip them all off, ideally in one rapid shot. People on the applied end of a zipper describe this as a lightning bolt of sensation or a fucking rush, depending on how long the pins have been left on. The reason for using four or five is that you want the pins to be pulled away as perpendicular to the body as possible and from both sides. Using more clothespins and yanking the cord from only one side can be more intense but raises the risk that some of the clothespins will twist, break, and rip the bottom's skin.

Again: *Ouch.*

And not in a good way.

If you do want to be evil (and I know you do), make more than a single set of zippers. Two, perhaps, for each breast with one on each side of the nipple. This way, you can yank one set off, wait a bit, then continue with the next. Repeat this to your heart's desire and your bottom's delightful yells.

Clothespins can also be quite fun on genitalia. But this is where it is extra important to use the type without teeth. A bit of skin torn from a breast is one thing, but having a divot of tissue torn from a labia or the underside of a cock is quite another.

For those with penis and testicles, clothespins can be placed on the scrotum and the underside of the shaft or, depending on the person's anatomy, the glans. As these areas can be extremely sensitive, it's important not to leave the clothespins on too long. Start slow and see what you can build up to.

For those with labia, clothespins can be placed, well, wherever they fit. Personally, I don't recommend the clitoris as that special little button could be damaged by excessive pressure, not to mention if a clothespin was applied and then suddenly jerked away.

As with anything in the BDSM world, learning as much as possible is not just a good idea but essential.

If my playful little chit-chat has you excited to try, don't run out to the dollar store and get dozens and dozens of these wonderful little devices until you've done your research. Take classes, read articles, watch videos, and repeat and repeat and repeat again and again. THEN give clothespins a shot.

One thing that is fantastic about clothespins, aside from their affordability, versatility, and intensity, is that they are an experience that can, and should, be shared.

Right up there with learning everything and anything—and always playing with safety (emotionally as well as physically) in mind—a good top should know what *everything* feels like. So try them on yourself.

There is no reason why anyone shouldn't be able to see how they feel coming, going, and zippered away. Afterward, fully armed with this knowledge, you'll be able to take the humble little clothespin out for a spin on other people.

CHAPTER 21:
Make Me A Lady, Lady With Ava Durda

In our roleplay section, we touched on dressing/acting as other genders. And you just read Chris' wonderful take on cross dressing, drag queens, etc. Another one of the special people we know, somebody who has worked hard to bring sexual positivity to all she meets, be you her friend, client, lover, is Ms. Ava Durda. At one time, Ava ran a very successful 'safe house' for men looking to enjoy cross-dressing and sissification, called The Sissy Parlor. Like a lot of places though, her wonderful spot didn't survive the pandemic, but Ava has been continuing her work coaching cross-dressing clients (and sometimes their partners) via phone and webcam. Working this way the lovely Ava is able to provide personalized expertise and support to CDs anywhere in the world, and at a much lower cost than in-person sessions. (Interested parties can find her here www.avadurga.com)

Ava really knows here stuff, as you will read below.

Q. How do you distinguish between the terms feminization and sissification...or do you at all?

Like many labels, I think they mean whatever someone wants them to mean. I've never found a consensus online or among my clients to use one over the other. I personally think of feminization as a catch-all term that can apply to any activity involving males wearing women's garments or adopting female mannerisms, and consider sissies a special subset that are hyper-feminine and more submissive, with over-the-top clothing (pink satin maid uniforms, streetwalker attire, etc.) and a stronger dose of humiliation. Sissy is an emotionally loaded word for most men. And although many of my clients don't identify as sissies, they don't fret over the semantics, so neither do I.

Proving what we have said all along in that, when you are 'in' a thing, engaging mind, body, spirit, and have a partner with you who had your back, no matter what it is you might be wearing on your back, you can call what you do and what you ate anything you like. You make the rules, meter out the definitions, it's an individual distinction and that's what most matters.

Now, for some, simply dressing in women's clothing is the nadir of the kink or diversion, for others, dressing in what they feel is 'feminine' is only the beginning of what other folks might be after.

The most common requests I get are for slut training and bi fantasy play. A fascination with cocks other than their own, cum, and stockings, too, are on the top of the list of what my clients often ask for," Ava informs us of what she has experienced beyond just a client dressing up..

Q. So, how did a nice girl like you...

A. In my mid-40s, I was hired as an office manager (think BDSM dungeon den mother) for a large commercial dungeon in Fort Lauderdale (up until that time, my life was pretty vanilla). Though my role was to hire and manage the Mistresses and houseboys and to screen clients. I wasn't a session Mistress. I took the same training and participated in sessions upon request. There were quite a few of those requests, which felt marvelous because I was a lot older than the staff.

My favorite clients and houseboys were the sissies and cross-dressers. Many of them had bi fantasies, too, which I really enjoy. There's something about gender-bending that intrigued me even then, and I found most of these men to be sweeter, more interesting, more playful, more self-aware, and more fun for me than the typical BDSM client. I also became their confidante, and the common themes I heard made my heartache (and sometimes made me angry). Good, loyal men rejected by partners for expressing this simple and harmless desire, chronic fear of discovery, heaps of societal shame, worries about sexual orientation, and the buy-guilt-purge cycle.

In the years since my involvement in kink and human sexuality has waxed and waned due to other responsibilities and relationship dynamics. Around 2011 I launched a project called Creative Sexuality Education. Although no longer up and running, it was a website and online campus for sex educators to teach online classes, dormant now because of resource limitations. The opportunity to network and take classes and webinars with experts contributed a lot to my knowledge and professional development. Continuing education and personal development are extremely important to me.

When my relationship ended, I became free to develop fully as a dominant woman and discover what works for me. What I discovered was a natural affinity and talent for working with men *en femme* and those with gender-bending and bisexual fantasies.

I decided to go pro after a long conversation at the Beyond Leather conference (beyondleather.net) with Lady Q, the Headmistress of ClubFem Southeast Florida (HOME | clubfemseflorida) and a retired prodomme who was nationally known for her work with sissies and cross-dressers. Lady Q recognized my interests and aptitude, encouraged me to go into professional practice, and has since become a valued mentor, friend, and cheerleader for The Sissy Parlor.

Q. This is a specific service you provide?

A. Yes, I cater to a specific niche and limit my practice to activities I really like: bi and femme fantasy, cross-dressing and sissification, basic makeovers, domestic service and discipline, corporal punishment, sissy slut and sissy maid training, sensory exploration, and being a supportive female coach offering companionship and advice to my clients exploring their sexuality while in my care.

I also like foot worshipers because it feels SO good, and littles, adult babies, and furries because they're precious and fun.

Phone sessions and coaching are another fast-growing part of my business. There are men all over the country who want someone intelligent to confide in and help them explore. They can tell that I care and am dialed into their interests and concerns.

Q. What don't you do at the parlor?
A. I'm not a leather domme or sadist, so I don't engage in things like extreme pain, blood, scat, spitting, smoking, ball-busting, punching, complicated or extended bondage, sounds, branding, scrotal inflation, breath play, etc. I also don't session topless, allow body worship above the knee, or do anything ending in shower or job. There's nothing wrong with those activities, just not my style.

Q. From our forays to kink conventions and writing about adult stuff, we find the kinky among us the most normal people one could ever meet. Do your clients come from straight backgrounds? Would you say they are coming to you to indulge in a fantasy or take a mental vacation from their lives mostly?
Yes. All of my clients identify as straight or selectively bisexual. They're generally professionally successful, mannerly, intelligent, often happily married family men, and mature (ages 45–75+). Seriously, the nice person next door.

Most tell me they've fantasized about feminization or bi play throughout their lives. Many already experiment in secret, but I also get quite a few first-timers. Almost all say the desire is getting stronger as they mature. (I have a few hunches about why that is, but am still gathering info).

It's hard to parse out the difference between indulging a fantasy and a mental escape. Some just enjoy the tactile pleasures of wearing lingerie. Some are turned on by seeing themselves as a different gender (*autogynephilia*). Some are exploring their own gender identity. Some fantasize about sucking cock. Some want to serve as a maid. Some love feeling like a sexy, receptive, desirable woman or a wanton slut.

In whatever form, they take off their tough man-cloak at my front door, and I bring them into a softer, more sensual alternative reality where they can live out fantasies that might be too risky to get elsewhere.

Q. Can you take us through a typical session?
A. Of course it varies by client, but I commonly start by dressing him in lingerie, stockings, makeup, wig, shoes, and accessories, then walk him to the full-length mirror. When he opens his eyes and sees himself fully *en femme*, often for the first time, it's exhilarating for us both. They're usually mesmerized, run their hands over their body, feel the different shapes and textures, look into their own eyes and see a new aspect of themselves. I can feel their energy change. It's hot to watch.

Some don't want full feminization or makeup. Garters and stockings or silky panties alone may do the trick. Or sexy heels. Or a nightgown.

From there, lots of things can happen. Fantasy fulfillment, sensation play or discipline, maid or slut training, girl talk, trying other outfits, etc. It depends on their goals for the experience.

Q. Lots of dominants claim to do this kind of session; how does what you do differ?

A. Aside from the fact that I specialize in feminization and bi fantasy (rather than it being one item on a long menu of dungeon activities), I've been told that I have a calm, reassuring manner and an intuitive understanding of what my clients need. Some have found it hard to connect with Mistresses who are young, coarse, or intimidating, or who work in a place with a dark dungeon-ey vibe.

The Parlor is in an elegant domestic setting. I'm in my fifties and share many of the same life experiences — corporate career, family pressures, life transitions — but have also experiences and social circles they only dream of. To some, I represent a sexier, more playful, more accepting, more open-minded version of the women in their lives. To others, I'm stricter and more exotic but still take good care of my pets. In either case, it's apparent that I care and love my work. All these things put them at ease and produce a memorable experience.

CHAPTER 22:
All Tied Up, No Place to Go

On Safe Bondage

From a partner holding their lover's hands behind their back to trussing-up a kinky player in a fuck-swing, there's a marvelous variety of methods for the kink-minded or the kink-wanting to tie on.

What's especially cool about bondage is that it isn't exclusively a kink for the uber-experienced. Beginners can forgo shopping at their local heavy-duty BDSM emporium. (Have you seen some of the stuff in those stores or online? It'll scare a newbie good!) Instead, scour your neighborhood hardware or grocery store for stuff to restrain someone.

But before you do anything, it's essential to make sure everyone involved is really, actually, truthfully willing. To this, remember the three big points of BDSM: safety, sanity, and consensuality. If you or your partner don't have every one of these, then stop, do not pass go, do not tie them up, or allow yourself to be restrained.

This is doubly so when playing with someone you don't know exceptionally well. While it isn't as said as loud as it should be, including in the BDSM community, bondage always brings with it a great deal of risk, up to and including permanent nerve damage and—no, we're not dramatic— possible *death.*

In short, *never* do anything bondage-related unless you know everything you possibly can about the risks involved, what to do should anything go wrong, and to play exclusively with people who communicate well, who are experienced, treat bondage with open-eyed awareness and concern for your well-being.

If you have any (and we mean *any*) concerns or doubts, don't play! Don't rush into anything if you don't feel 100% certain about what could happen.

Sure, we know it's hard to resist a whole room or salivating kinksters seemingly having the time of their lives or a new date who suddenly reveals they're into your just-only-ever-fantasized-about-kink. But no matter what it is you may get up to, always err on the side of playing with partners, be they lovers or even fuck-buds. You want to play with people you trust and who never fail to take responsibility and act accordingly if anything should go south. (And not south in a good way.)

After all, as it is with any kink, hell as with anything we do, jumping into the deep end of the bondage pool could get you drowned right quick!

So how does one get into being tied down or binding their lover?

What are the best items to use and how far should we take it all?

What are the dangers? What exactly is bondage? And are there other ways to get into this kink without using robes or chains?

Let's unravel (sorry, punsters we will forever be) this wacky fun activity known as bondage.

What NOT To Do, Part 1

Like everything, there is a wrong way, a right way, and room for exploration with bondage. The wrong way is pretty obvious. It's wrong if your bottom is in pain (not the good kind) or suffers some type of injury. A tried-and-true (or should we say *tied-and-true?*) BDSM maxim should be repeated here. The definitive test of any top isn't their play, or the tricks they know, but how they react when things go wrong.

With that in mind, never fail to approach your bondage activities with an eye towards Murphy's Law and be aware of what the human body can and cannot take.

Really kids, throughout this book, we've erred on the side of maximum safety in whatever you get into. With this bondage stuff, though, as you'll come to see, we aren't kidding!

As we said above, bondage is *dangerous*. The human body, after all, can be remarkably fragile, especially around the wrists and ankles, knees and elbows, and the neck. Put the wrong kind or an undue amount of pressure on any of these body parts, and you risk cutting off circulation (if you're lucky) or suffering permanent nerve damage (if you're not) or worse, suffocation and—as we noted before—*death*.

So, let's begin by touching on that #1 no-no spot, the big place on our bodies to avoid playing with bondage, the neck. *Do not put anything, anything at all, against the throat.* Now, the back of the neck is fine, but you want to avoid placing any kind of pressure against the windpipe for apparent reasons (um, like … *breathing*).

You've probably heard of *erotic asphyxiation,* which is done by either hanging, playing with choking, or through other means of cutting off someone's (or your own) air supply.

Please, please, *please* leave this pursuit alone!

Erotic asphyxiation doesn't even fall into the "If you're into that sort of thing" category, as the odds are that you or someone else is gonna die. And if a mishap does not immediately, then it might sometime in the future. Also, avoid genital or breast bondage. Yes, you might see or read of plenty of kinksters into this kind of a thing, but if you're a first-timer, stay away from anything complicated involving your lover's chest or genitals.

The *why* behind our warning is that those areas are extra fragile, more so than joints, and though no one (as far as we know) has died from bondage in these areas, there's still a high probability that those anatomical fun zones will be irreparably damaged.

Onto the joints: stay clear of restriction on or around the wrists, elbows, ankles, or knees.

Why? Because even the slightest pressure applied to them in the wrong way, or for too long, may result in everything from temporary discomfort all the way to permanent nerve damage!

If the person restrained feels cold/cool or has any kind of numbness/tingling that's an immediate sign that the bondage is too tight and *they should be released immediately!*

This is why what you use for bondage and where you put it is also vital. Which just happens to be coming up shortly.

What NOT To Do, Part 2

If you're getting sick of us belaboring safety… well, *too fucking bad!*

We're not trying to pour ice water on your steamy fantasies but to open your eyes. Though bondage can be hot, bondage can be arousing, bondage—as we said and will keep on saying—*bondage is risky!*

As with kink play of any sort, before anything happens, establish a safeword.

Think of it this way. You're in the middle of some amazingly heated sexual act and moaning.

"No, no stop, oh no…not that!"

Your partner misinterprets this. Your partner thinks you are having a good time. They might think that all that no pleading stuff is just you reacting, trying to be combative so as to prompt them to give more.

To eliminate this kind of confusion, to make sure your top exactly knows what you mean, the two of you need establish a *safeword*. It should be something you'd not usually say, like *elephant*. Deciding on this word before play will allow you to communicate that you aren't presently enjoying yourself. In other words, it clearly establishes that you really do want things to stop right now.

If a bottom says 'the word' all action stops!

With bondage, things can take a turn for the worst at a moment's notice. Clear communication is critical, especially if your bondage scene includes blindfolds, and certainly gags

But how can they signal to their top when they can't say anything? Answer: by holding an object in their hand and dropping it they can let their top know that something's not right and that everything should *immediately* stop

And since we just mentioned gags….please use high-quality gags only and never anything that restricts a person's ability to breathe or communicate. Do *not* pick up anything from your local porn shop or a fly-by-night website. Never make do with anything you have on hand like socks or stockings. We are all too serious here, to the tune of far too many people have fatally suffocated due to the use of poorly-constructed, impromptu gags from impromptu gags.

In fact, overall, it's a damn good idea to regularly check in with anyone who's restrained. A big what not to do, and unfortunately something we hear horror stories about constantly, is someone leaving their trussed-up partner alone.

Let's repeat this last bit...

Please NEVER, EVER, LEAVE YOUR ANYONE THIS WAY.

No matter what, always stay with the person you have put into bondage. Again, anything can happen at any time. The briefest moment away from a bottom could have, and has had tragic consequences. (We have heard too many horror stories.)

Your Bondage Emergency Kit

So, you've read the cautions about what *not* to do, now we can talk about *what to do* or, more precisely, what to have on hand when tying someone up or when restrained yourself.

Bondage Emergency Basics:

You should always have a pair of safety emergency shears. These allow you to cut someone out of most materials without the risk of injuring them with a sharp edge. While a cheap set will do in a pinch, it's worth investing in a stronger pair which can cut through practically *everything*.

But don't bury these into your play-bag. Instead, have them at the ready at all times. We would even go so far as to suggest hanging them on a lanyard around your neck or wrapping the handles with glow tape. That way, if they fall or you forget them in your play bag, you can spot them, even in the low light of a BDSM playspace.

You should practice using your scissors. You want to be, no, *need to be*, good enough to cut whatever you might be using in a fraction of a second. Time truly counts in bondage play. If there is any, absolutely *any* sign of distress or discomfort, put these scissors to work. After all, it's better to be safe than sorry, especially when sorry can lead to serious injury. Another crucial basic piece of bondage safety gear are Panic Snaps (also sometimes called Quick Release Snaps). Picture a durable metal clasp held shut by an easily-slidable sheath so rather than having to lift or move a possibly unconscious person all you need to do is slide it up and, viola, it releases. With a a Quick Release Snap at every point in a bondage scene, you can get someone out of it faster than you could with emergency scissors.

Bondage Emergency Essentials:

In addition to basic bondage safety tools like Safety Shears and Panic Snaps, absolutely must-have *emergency gear* begins with having plenty of water at the ready to prevent dehydration and, if the scene is arousing, compensating for any fluids the restrained person might be expelling if the scene is particularly ... exciting.

However, don't drink so much that the person bound will have to pee in the middle of the bondage session—unless, of course, you're into that sort of thing.

Naturally, if either of you has any critical medications — allergies, diabetes, etc.— your usual pills or something like a protein bar is a must-have in your play bag.

Last but not least-ly: *have your phone on you!* Not to sound like a broken record, but again, time is critical in a bondage emergency, so you should *never* hesitate to call for assistance beyond yelling out for a dungeon monitor if you're playing in a public space.

Yeah, you might be a little embarrassed, and we all know how dungeons frown on cell phone use, but a quick call could be a real lifesaver.

The Dope on Rope Here's where we get unpopular, notably with more than a few members of the BDSM community, but let's face facts: *don't use rope for bondage!*

"What…"

We hear those kinky people and everyone else who has been seduced by all those Shibari videos (elaborate demonstrations of one person tying up another using the ancient art of Japanese rope bondage or "kinbaku") that too often seem to be the only thing that comes up when searching about bondage.

"What are you saying?"

Read our lips. *Rope should only be used by experts with years of experience.* Even then, there remains the possibility that someday, something awful might happen. The harsh reality is that rope, being inflexible and narrow, can easily damage joints. Worse, getting someone out of a Shibari-type scene, even with Emergency Scissors or when utilizing Panic Snaps, takes too much time.

And time, as we say over and over again, something no one can afford to waste in a bondage crisis.

So, repeat with us please. "I will not use rope for bondage!"

"But then… what should I use to restrain someone?"

We hear you.

Vet Wrap

Allow us to present the wonder of the bondage world: Vet Wrap, also called Self-Adhesive Bandages. This comfortably-spongy stuff is easily wrapped around a person's wrists and, because it's several inches wide, won't put undue pressure on their joints. Plus, it can be twisted into sometime akin to a short length of effortlessly cuttable cord or tied to a Quick Release Snap for extra-added safety in case of an emergency.

Plastic Wrap

Have you ever hear Mel Brooks and Carl Reiner's *2000 Year Old Man* comedy shtick?

No?

What is the world coming to… (sigh).

Anyway, in that bit, Mel, you guessed it, plays a 2000-year-old man. When asked by Carl, playing a reporter, to name the single greatest invention in the history of mankind, Mel replies: "Plastic wrap!"

Not to take away from a pair of comedy legends, but what they say in jest can be said for bondage. Plastic wrap can be great for restraining someone.

Here's how it works. Get your bottom naked and standing at the foot of a relatively high bed. Futons are NOT recommended. You'll see why in a second.

Next, take your plastic wrap and begin to wrap them. A good idea is to start high on the body, go round the chest and slowly work down. This way, they'll have the use of their legs for balance.

After working your way down, you can then *carefully* lower your subject onto the bed, being sure not to drop them and not to allow their head to smack into anything.

It's important not to cover the person's face or go too many times around with the wrap. Three or so is fine as it shouldn't restrict their breathing too much.

As for what kind of plastic wrap to use, the cooking variety is preferred as it's designed to trap a degree of heat and moisture inside. The *degree* part is why it's a favorite. Industrial wrap, often used in packaging and such, isn't at all permeable, exacerbating the big concern about this kind of play: *body heat*. When one is wrapped, in any material, or even slightly covered, one's body temperature rises. This might indeed be what the players want, so have it surely. But the person wrapping their lover like yummy leftovers, needs to always be aware of how much the wrap-ess body heat is rising and if mere naughty sexual discomfort isn't becoming possible heat prostration. Depending on the person who is under/wrapped or otherwise restricted by a material, etc. body temperature can rise rather quickly and create some real problems.

This is why cooking wrap is better, it doesn't really 'roasting,' anyone wrapped in it. Still you need to keep a keen eye on your bottom and listen closely to what they are saying about the heat level.

If you or your new mummy have never engaged in plastic wrap fun before, leave the wrap on for no longer than five or so minutes. This all depends on the heat in the room as well as how hot your bottom runs generally.

Another benefit to plastic wrap, aside from being cheap and easy to apply. It's also easy to have a comfortable bondage experience and even easier removal, just take your Emergency Shears and zzziiipppp them out of it. With a bit of practice, this can be done in a few seconds.

Latex Tape

Latex Tape can be another alternative bondage tool. Like with Vet Wrap, Latex Tape sticks to itself and, if it is wide enough, can be used without putting too much pressure on joints.

It can also be quickly removed with your trusty Emergency Scissors. The only drawback to latex tape is its cost, especially compared to Plastic Wrap or Vet Wrap. But it does look really sexy and comes in a whole range of glossy, neat-o colors.

* * * *

Use your imagination BDSM can also be fertile ground for your kinky imagination, and even more so with bondage. So let's put our deviously-kink minds together and think of some unique ways to keep someone from moving.

Like placing a bunch of teeny little paper cups filled with water along their prone body and telling them that, heaven forbid, any of them spill, bait or receive a caning or flogging while 'holding' the water. Ah, the imagination soars...

Not into water, then how about loosely tying bells to their ankles, wrists, around their waist or anywhere else that might be fun, again with the promise of punishment if any of them should ring.

Moving without moving

Finally, we have a form of bondage that is both completely safe and potentially extremely intense, and requires no supplies or safety gear.

Your partner is on a bed or sitting in a chair or standing. You tell them, in your best growl, that this method of restraint will test the limits of their endurance and self-control.

Next comes the all-important part.

You instruct them: "Don't move."

Sometimes called *Honor Bondage*, this elegant game can be challenging to even the most experienced bottoms. If it isn't a challenge, you can make it more interesting by throwing ping-pong balls at them, or spraying ice water, or very carefully, *please*, applying hot wax.

Don't forget to negotiate any and all of the above and everything else you might be doing beforehand. Sure, these ideas above might seem like simple forms of play. Still, until you talk with the person involved about your plans, you could be unintentionally causing a great deal of emotional discomfort.

It's true in life and even more so with BDSM. *Never assume anything!*

* * * *

Remember that though bondage is a common and arousing form of sex play, it is also one of kink's highest risk activities.

Because of this, safety shouldn't be only on your mind but the first and last thing you think about. If *anything* happens during a scene, including if you're unsure things are going well or you feel communication isn't as straightforward as it should be, never hesitate to get your subject out of what you've put them into.

CHAPTER 23:
"Have I Really Been *That* Bad?!"

Spanking 101

Far be it for us or anyone else to tell anyone what they should do during their sexual explorations. Hell, if a single theme is clear to you after reading this book, it should be that we're deadly serious that whatever you want to get into is your business. As long as it's consensual.

There are people who begin their first expedition into the world of non-vanilla naughtiness by buying their first flogger or cane, or maybe trying a little role-play. For many, their initial foray into kink sex play is via *spanking*.

Yes, plenty of us have exchanged the ubiquitous love tap to/with/from a partner or playfully given or taken a birthday swatting from a friend. But spanking, for fun and profit, can be so much more. Swatting a lover's behind, be it bare, be it with hand or implement, can be an A+, number one turn on.

So, bend over, and let's get to it.

The Where, The How, And The Why

Since there isn't much more to spanking than meeting your hand with someone's bottom, you can pretty much do it anywhere. However, if you want a more extended session or one that might see some bared booty (or even an orgasm or two) probably some seclusion to the session is best. Dropping trough and bending over someone's lap at the next family barbecue might just be pushing past the bounds of propriety, even if old Aunt Katy would love to watch. (Aunt Katy always was a bit of a scamp.)

A side note ... as many couples get off on the humiliation aspect of spanking (that old over-the-knee position does bring back childhood memories for many), we have it on good authority (we really do such extensive research for you, don't we?) that many a spanker and spank-ee enjoy having their swatting witnessed by others. But please, do not expose your sexual desires (or anything else) to anyone who hasn't consented to being a witness.

Alone then or with others, you could undoubtedly execute a spanking with the receiver bent across any chair, table, or kitchen countertop. Across one's lap is also a premium position and considered a classic, so much so it is known by those into this kink by that OTK abbreviation.

The actual *ways* of conducting a spanking—the position everyone gets into, implements used, and techniques—are multitudinous. (Seriously, how often does one get to use the word *multitudinous*?) So, the real concern here is over severity.

As with every activity we've explored, those involved must consistently communicate with each other. Partners can determine a true *STOP* from a faux one. (Come up with those safewords or agree on a physical movement that indicates a complete ceasing of all action.)

Case in point: you may have fantasized for decades about how much you want to feel a wooden spoon bouncing off your ass (it should come as no surprise that for many with a spanking Jones, everyday household items fix deeply in their fantasies), but what happens when one or two smacks from this usually innocent kitchen item suddenly feels too intense? What is felt has a lot to do with what's used, ranging from a stinging bottom that goes numb after a time, flaming cheeks blushed and bruised, and so forth. So, keep in mind… instruments employed coupled with how hard they are used, and where, make the difference, for sure. For instance, smacking the backs of someone's thighs raises a quicker sting than if you were to smack the meatier center-area of the buttocks, often referred to as the *sweet spot*.

And while someone lying draped across your knees will feel an excellent right smack when you connect your hand, and certainly more so your wood-backed hairbrush to their ass, imagine how much more intense this could be if the spank-ee is grabbing their ankles— pulling their body taut and presenting a much more tensed and possibly clenched glutinous to their spanker.

And don't think that you can't do hard-hitting with merely an open hand because you definitely can. The thing is, though, spanker and spank-ee will both begin to smart after a few minutes, typically with the spanker calling safeword first as the human hand is far more sensitive and fragile than your fun-of-the-mill ass.

It might mean much more

Sexual fantasies made real often bubble forth with a bunch of deep stuff you and your partner may have kept hidden or were never aware of. It may spew from the depths of your psyches. Spanking, which, while getting endorphins rushing, can also set off emotional triggers.

Many of us, especially of a specific generation, were spanked when we were kids. Though these memories might be the very last thing on your mind when considering this kink or when lying across a lover's lap, sometimes, shit happens! Given this, while role-play—teacher/student, auntie/nephew-niece, employer/boss, and so forth—can be part and parcel of kink play, a special caution should be taken during a spanking session because of what the whole action could bring to the surface from when somebody was spanked in their real life years before. It might seem a small point to you, it only takes one specific experience prior to what is supposed to be spanking fun, be it the spanker or spankee, and it could be something simple like saying, "No, Daddy/Mommy, no more please," to snap heretofore unknown chords in a bottom's or top's brain. It could unexpectedly spin all kinds of mental wheels in ways no one ever expected. Even when either of both parties wanted the role-play, the naughty talk, and/or labels used.

A further note about things said during play, when spanking or partaking in anything else.

Once and for all, be it kinky or not, involving stuffed llamas and pith helmets or chocolate sauce... (We really hit the chocolate sauce hard here, haven't we?) Let's all please admit, here and now, that lots of the words uttered don't mean much beyond their utterance during sex playtime. Plenty of bottoms have moaned a "No, Daddy," but they aren't thinking of their parents as the full heat of their libido is coaxed to a full flame.

It's one of those little snigletts of sex we think bears repeating.

Quite often the thing is just what it is when it is said or done and nothing more.

Sure, we have just proved in the few paragraphs above, how it might not be (if spanking triggers deeper memories and feelings) but lots of times, most times — a thing is just the thing...Gertrude Stein.

* * * *

To the actual *how to* land a swat, no matter how hard you want to give or get and regardless of how often you have enjoyed spanking, here are significant points of caution for getter and giver:

For the spanker

Aim mainly for the spank-ee's *sweet spot* as mentioned above. This is the meatiest part of the buttocks, from the fullest part at its top to where the upper thighs folds into the bottom.

Universally, stay well away from too high or too low. The former is the land of the kidneys, and you don't ever want to damage those critical organs. The latter is close to the tailbone, or coccyx, in other words, the base of the spine. Particularly obey this when employing an implement, as you could do unexpectedly excessive damage and not realize it.

Conversely, and again hitting with anything other than your hand, you may see redness or initial bruising while not harming them at all.

Again, communication is critical. Listen to what your partner is saying, as in how much it smarts or if they want things to smart more.

Generally, it's a good idea to warm your partner up first. Unless you're explicitly doing punishment play, with the idea to make the spanking intense from the get-go, most players like to start things off slower/gentler.

Getting an ass rosy and warm from a light hand spanking, then moving up, in either intensity or in what's used to make those smacks, usually assures the spanking play will go on for a good and arousing, long time.

* * * *

For Spank-ee

As we just said, what seems to be happening visually across your ass is not necessarily what's happening regarding the severity of what you're feeling.

So, it's your responsibility to clue your spanker into how you're feeling. This is especially important when playing with someone for the first time. Better to break a mood than get needlessly hurt because you were playing at being the stoic little bottom.

Once put in a position, try your best not to roll or shuck out of it. Too many people shift unexpectedly around, move a swatting, or involuntarily thrust a hand behind themselves to ward off a hit and end up getting hit in not-very-arousing places.

Now as to the *why* of a spanking. Here comes the eternal question of discipline versus arousal in this kink. As much as it is impossible to advise on the where and the how, beyond the simple suggestions we've made, nobody will ever be able to advise you and yours on the *reason* for spanking.

It may be as simple as a couple who enjoy a light spanking session (or at least one of the partners does) now and again. Spanking can be about getting off on the sexual stimulation, and that's all.

Other times spanking can be a disciplinary measure, something those involved worked out beforehand. In this case, the spanking is not really taking on a sexual aspect in and of itself. The punishment spanking is usually more about power exchange—something we haven't really spoken about.

Bottom line, pun intended, you'll find what works best for you and your partner. Sometimes you'll find one reason works one time, while at another, a new motivation or implement prompts you.

The point is, there are fewer ways to give and get a spanking than there are reasons behind wanting to play. As long as everything's consensual and you and those who play with come out the other side feeling better than when you went in then that's *wonderful!*

CHAPTER 24:
Hurts so Good

A Short, Quick Guide to Sensual Caning and Rhythm Play

"Are you ready, Worthless Slut?"

Mistress Nastina growled with disgust, tapping one of her finest birching rods in the palm of one of her shapely, though frighteningly strong, hands.

"Y-Y-yes, Mistress," the quivering bottom kneeling before her answered.

"Then it is time for you to receive PUNISHMENT!"

Nastina hissed, a serpent preparing to strike, the cane arcing down with a blurring, moaning sweep towards the pale, gleaming ass…

* * * *

Whoa! Just hang on there a second, Mistress!

More than any other BDSM activity, caning has perhaps the greatest gap between serious enjoyment and literary depictions.

Go after someone with a "blurring, moaning sweep," and you're not going to have a delighted bottom, but rather a pissed-off one screaming their safeword louder than an opera singer with their genitals in a mousetrap.

To be fair, the real way to enjoy a stiff birch (or plastic or rattan or bamboo) rod isn't all that … well, dramatic.

Instead, a delicate, rhythmic tapping is the way to proceed.

Let's talk first about basic safety. As this book has reminded us, that is the first concern whenever we talk about or get familiar with any form of BDSM play. It is especially important where caning is involved. As in spanking, hitting someone with a long, thin rod requires knowing *where* to do your striking as there are as many good places to strike as no-no zones.

As you may have assumed here, the ass—nature's joy-buzzer—is the primo piece of real estate for caning, especially the afore-explored sweet spot.

Like with spanking, though much more with caning, if you hit that sweet spot with a rhythmic beat, the bottom gets their genitals nicely thrummed as well, via the sympathetic vibrations through the fatty, muscular portions of their ass.

And finding the right can be fun as materials are varied, sometimes organic (rattan, bamboo, or similar), sometimes not (acrylic or other plastics).

Sometimes the cane is not technically a cane (riding crop, rug beater, switch from the backyard).

Unlike other impact toys (such as a flogger, belt, or paddle), canes shouldn't be employed across someone's back, though, yes, sometimes people prefer that they be used there. But as should be clear (though we'll make it even clearer), the number one no-no impact spot, the should-NEVER-be-hit-zone, is the spine. Even a glancing blow to it, intentionally or otherwise, can cause damage.

Some people also play on the thighs. Still, we suggest a much less aggressive attack there are there is the potential risk of injury. Butts, remember, evolved as a cushion, thighs not so much.

Suffice it to say that unless you happen to be in a Turkish prison, the bottom of the feet or palms of the hands is also *nowhere* you want to go with a rod.

So we've got the turf staked out: aim for the ass, paying particular attention to stay away from the spine, the base of the spine, and the kidneys. (Put your hands behind your back. That's where they are.) Now you need a weapon of choice.

As mentioned, canes come in two primary breeds, natural and not. The differences can be worlds apart. Organic canes are cheap, readily available, and can be on the slightly lower end of the sensation scale (though this depends on a lot of factors).

Artificial canes are generally a lot more expensive, harder to find, and are on the higher end of that ouch! meter.

The big difference between the two is cleanliness. Unexpectedly, caning can result in a bit of blood being raised or exuded (usually from popping a zit or a quick cut). This is important as organic canes can't be sterilized, even when they've been varnished.

 • The rule in these instances is when you bleed on a wooden toy, you own it. Plastic, though, often *can* be effectively cleaned.

 • The intensity a toy brings to a person's ass is dependent on all kinds of things: material,

 • thinness (the thinner, the more of a sting it can create) weight (heavier equaling bruising and more of a thuddy sensation) spring or acceleration (faster resulting in more of a "bite").

Thus, a thin, heavy plastic cane will foster more of a sharp pain than, say, a thick, light, wooden one. Choose your weapon with care, as what you pull from the bag can have a major effect on your bottom's bottom.

Now onto use.

Once again, leave Mistress Nastina on the bookshelf where they belong. Unless you're going for pure punishment strokes, the best way to use a cane is like a fast, steady metronome to employing those *delicate, rhythmic, tapping* strokes.

Here's a great exercise to learn how to do just this. Take a pencil or chopstick and smack your thigh once like the fearsome Mistress Nastina does. Then, instead try to build up a Buddy Rich drum solo or like Animal from The Muppets. Pick the reference best suited to your generation.

You'll quickly find a Mistress Nastina stroke is closer to Mean Ass Mistress, with the Buddy Rich tapping definitely more pleasurable.

Remember, drama is the spice, but the pudding is endorphins. The best way of raising them is rhythmic tapping— slowly rising in intensity over a given period of time.

* * * *

One of the hardest things to learn about using a cane is how to make the damned thing behave. Take your new toy (plastic or natural), hold the handle, and steadily move your wrist to get it waving up and down. You want just enough force to get the tip moving a foot or so.

After a few seconds, you'll notice that the cane is flying all over the place. Now, turn the handle a little bit and try again. After a few turns, you'll find a place where the cane will go straight up and down with little or no oscillations. This is the cane's balance point. This is where you'll be able to control where it goes.

You have to watch out for *wrapping*, where the tip of the toy falls beyond the curve of the ass and thus accelerates much faster than the rest of the cane, snapping around and–you guessed it–*wrapping*. This also occurs with floggers.

The symptoms of this happening are usually apparent to you, and certainly to your bottom. A split-second gap between an enjoyable impact on the fatty tissue of the butt and a welt-raising *Pop* as the end of the toy speeds up. The solution is easy, though. Pull back on the cane so that the end impacts on the old sweet spot and not beyond it.

Also, note that the final two or three inches of the cane should be impacting whoever you're playing with and not less. Striking with only the tip can frequently be way too intense for most people.

Let's talk rhythm. With caning (as with flogging), try to keep up a regular beat (*and a one, two, three, four*). Striking with a staggered, irregular impact can be jarring to those on the receiving end. Jarring also means it can be more challenging to enjoy.

Sure, you can play with different beats or strike harder or lighter during a single session. But first, you have to pump up those natural opiates with a good, sensual build-up of consistent smacks, just like in our spanking warm-up.

After the bottom has been guided upwards by your careful drumming on their *tuchus*, you can then lengthen the time between strokes. You can also make them harder/softer, and so forth, but try to never lose your timing.

Now that you've learned the basics lets talk about what happens afterward. Canes can be nasty suckers, even when used lightly. Untreated canes have been known to produce splinters that can easily escape detection at the start of a scene–and can draw blood.

If you draw blood during a caning scene, don't freak out. Just clean the wound, put a Band Aid on it, and toss the cane. Only clean it if it's plastic.

Canes can additionally cause bruises or welts. Neither is dangerous though might smart afterward. For bruising, Vitamin E cream followed by a routine of heat then ice will typically bring the swelling down.

Something else that comes up with people who like to *go natural* with their cane is that a top might have their bottom go out and cut their own switches. This can be a lot of fun, but don't forget that natural can also mean *dirty* or *allergenic*.

Our best advice here is to stick to store-bought and treated. No scene is worth a nasty infection or worse.

* * * *

There it is, folx. Our Short, Quick Guide to Sensual Caning.

Go forth, take up a nice rod, and have fun. Just don't tell Mistress Nastina we said.

CHAPTER 25:
Send In The Kinksters

How to find your neighborhood dungeon ... and what to do when you get there.

Looking for where kinksters mix and mingle to get their BDSM-beats on?

Want to explore showing off your play while taking in what others are doing as well?

Craving the companionship and support of people who are as delightfully, wonderfully twisted as you are?

Then, get thee to a dungeon.

Yes, you read that right.

Dungeon.

It might not be the hot spot where all the kids hang out, or even know about, and you're definitely not going to find one at the strip mall.

But if you're inclined to court a fetish or two and have a penchant for leather and stockades, or if you want to enjoy exercising voyeurism every now and again, then looking for like-minded kinksters at your local playspace could be the right place for you.

So put on your leather corset. Stick a ball-gag in your mouth. Clip that fashionable yet effective cat o' none tails to your belt.

We're off to find the dungeon of your dreams.

Finding the space

Dungeons rarely advertise existence, at least publicly. They are not typically taverns or high-energy rave clubs bursting with cars and people on a Saturday night. But go a-looking, and you just might find one.

Considering the size of your 'burb, there is most likely a dungeon near you waiting for you to visit. Whether it's the basement of somebody's house, a makeshift torture chamber in an industrial space rented once a month from a liberal landlord, or an actual 24/7 playspace, dungeons *are* out there.

First, check BDSM sites like Fetlife or peruse an appropriate Subreddit. If that doesn't work, you can do some Facebook investigating. Be you so bold, approach someone you see every now at your Starbucks who sports that heavy neck chain, the one the padlock.

If you're a novice and *have* located such a space, don't show up uninvited. Frequently these spaces require a reservation or you have to be a member of the group or club.

A great way to get that introduction, as well as an excellent way to connect with your local BDSM community, is to first attend some Munches.

Munches are casual get-togethers where kinky folk, or those interested in being introduced to kinky folk, meet to *munch* in a spot like the back room of a diner or the basement room of a tavern to break bread and jaw for a few hours.

Typically, munches discourage playing, so don't show up expecting a full-blown BDSM event. Same, too, with how you should dress. Think your typical clothes, not your full kink regalia.

Hopefully, at these kinds of meetups, you'll meet your fellows. Maybe you'll engage with someone you might play with later. And you can chat with people who might invite you to a dungeon party. Once you get to know them, they'll share locations and get-together times.

Respecting the space

You've been invited. Or maybe you made a date to meet someone. Even better, you joined a group. Whichever way, you've gathered enough facts about what to expect. You've finally steeled your nerve.

You make your first solo foray to a dungeon.

What should you expect? And, more importantly, what's expected of you?

As mentioned, many dungeons are members-only. Sometimes you can join at the door. Whether the dungeon you're entering is a make-shift affair in someone's big screened-in porch, a photographer's garage converted every third Wednesday night of the month, or an actual loft space delineated specifically for kink play six nights a week (one night off for hosing down), each space will probably charge a minimum fee to pay for snacks, lube, clean-up, staffing, etc.

Each dungeon has specific rules for safety and etiquette. These rules are to be obeyed, without question, just as you should respect the limits of someone you're playing with.

Since a dungeon is filled with people doing their own thing, or doing it a hell of a lot wilder than they do in most aspects of their life, the parameters in which people play and how a dungeon wants that play conducted are paramount. Though spaces have their own set of rules, there are sure to be a few tried-and-true ones that most dungeons will demand you follow.

No pictures. Please, please, please refrain from pulling out the old iPhone and snapping pics or video. People who come to dungeons to play in public do so because they know what happens there stays there. In fact, spaces have been known to ask that you either leave your phone at home or secure it in a provided locker. If you *can* bring it with you, absolutely keep it switched off or at the very least *silenced*.

Look, but don't touch ... unless you're invited to.

The thrill for lots of people who play in front of other people is that they are *playing in front of other people*. Couples, single folx, triads, and everyone else often using a playspace to take their playmates out for a stroll. For the most part, players shouldn't come to a dungeon unless they feel safe. Most enjoy some sort of voyeuristic or exhibitionist thrill. Feel free to look or to be looked at to your heart's content. BUT this doesn't mean lurking at anyone's elbow and gawking. Instead, maintain a respectful distance and do what you can to not interfere.

Never touch anyone or anything without explicit permission to do so. Dungeons, and the BDSM scene itself, is all about respect and tolerance. If you don't have either, then stay at home.

Listen to the DM.

The Dungeon Monitor (DM) is a dungeon's chief muckily-muck. They keep their eyes peeled for people misbehaving, leaping to help should a scene do bad. In general, they make sure things are safe for everyone there. Depending on the size of the space, a DM might have additional minions. They need to be obeyed—*period*. No one cares if you think you're the baddest, nastiest, and most Toppy of the Tops. When the DM tells you to do something or stop doing it, politely and respectfully comply. When if you don't agree with their methods or requests, they are the absolute authority. If you don't like that then, once again, just stay home.

Clean up after yourself.

While dungeons often provide the basics—sanitary wipes, disposable cloths, and condoms—put cleaning supplies in your playbag, as well.

Make use of all this before and especially after you've used the equipment. Not doing so will typically result in many bad looks and possibly even getting ejected from the space. For safety reasons and general politeness, whether you believe in a higher power or not, *cleanliness* is indeed next to *godliness*.

Don't get into an activity the dungeon doesn't support.

A quick rifle through your own naughty noggin' I'm sure would bring many possibilities to mind. Still, not everything you want to do is permissible in every dungeon.

Sure, people might be getting whipped, fisted, flogged, or bound up, but this doesn't mean *everything* goes. In most dungeons, water sports, electrical or wax play, or out-and-out sex, particularly the unprotected variety, usually won't be permitted.

But again, read the rules. Consult the dungeon's DM if you have to, or ask whoever's in charge. Asking will get you the lay of the land pretty fast for what's allowed and what isn't.

This ain't no disco.

A dungeon is not a dance club. Most never serve alcohol, though you can usually score bottled water or soft drinks for a minimal price. Music is also kept to a dull roar so people can enjoy the cries for mercy.

So don't get your boogie on or treat a dungeon like a pick-up joint. Yes, there's the possibility of meeting people to play with, but if you come on like an obnoxious pick-up artist (or should we say asshole), you're gonna get your ass kicked out.

No, uttered in a dungeon means *no*. Though you'll spy lots of people walking around wearing provocative clothing, or no clothing at all, this doesn't mean that person is amiable to you trying to chat them up. Kinky attire doesn't instant come-and-get-me make.

Be polite as if your status in the BDSM community is at stake, which it absolutely is. The BDSM scene tends to be very diligent at catching lousy behavior. Trouble makers get quickly back-balled from every party or gathering in the area and potentially, with the internet, everywhere else.

And if you do chat with someone, don't ever treat them as anything but an equal. While not necessarily as egregious as slobbering over someone or worse not taking no for an answer, fawning or commanding is a sure sign that a person doesn't understand that essential part of BDSM: *respect!*

The playspace/dungeon at a kink event

Suppose you have the dollars and can get away for a weekend. In that case, you might find the playspaces/dungeons/a delineated hotel ballroom outfitted for an event more to your liking.

But though people who come to a kink events are usually there for the same thing, or at least more liberal-minded than your usual round of pipe-fitter conventioneers (though, some of those folx can be wild, no doubt about it), typical dungeon rules apply to a kink event space.

One possible benefit is that it may not be as challenging to find a play partner at an event instead of at your local space, based on the sheer number of naughty players at a weekend get-away.

There's also how events can be way more focused, so if you're into anything from latex fashion to boot blacking there's a good chance there's a kink-fest out there with your name on it.

* * * *

They're out there: the playspaces, the kink events, the parties, and the dungeons. Finding them, and getting your feet wet in the BDSM pool, is only a matter of patience, tolerance, and respect.

Have those traits, and be willing to learn what the scene has to offer (and doesn't), and before you know it, you'll be an active and respected member of the scene.

CHAPTER 26:
Make Me Submit

How to find, engage and what to expect from a professional dominant (i.e. a for-pay top)

Lots of us foster thoughts, needs, and aches that we can't readily enlist a partner or lover into sharing. This is true for people new to BDSM as well as seasoned kinksters.

Now, paying a little extra for a happy finish with your massage or enlisting the services of that hunk sent to your room in Vegas is one thing, but trying to get your kink on with a professional dominant is an entirely different thing.

The internet pretty much killed those smaller art papers that used to appear in headshops and record stores (the 'net pretty much killed the need for headshops and record stores, too), so your only real option is to sally forth on your phone or laptop.

For now, Fetlife and its ilk are excellent sources of info and making social connections, as are the various dominant directories on the web. Escort review websites can help, too, though be cautioned that an escort who merely dabbles in domination won't compare with an actual, professional.

A benefit in searching online for a professional is that, after spending time getting the lay of the digital land, you can get pretty skilled about finding an ideal pro to scratch your particularly kinky itches.

That doesn't mean you can find someone on the web and jump right in, though. First you have to know how things *work*.

Lucky for you, that's where we come in!

Pre-Screening and Showing Up

Like with escorts, a professional dominatrix will insist on pre-screening. This can be done over the phone, with a few emails back and forth, or in their presence before the session begins.

No matter the process, you're likely going to have to hash out beforehand what you've come for and assure the professional that you're not a creep.

Lots of *service providers* ask for a reference, which is not easy to give if you're seeing someone for the first time. In other cases, they may ask for a trial session in a dungeon where other doms (and security) are present.

This is all about the dominant's safety. It's also a necessary precaution against getting busted, depending on local ordinances and the like. Typically, doms do not provide sexual services. Again, this all depends on the dominant as well as what the law will allow.

After convincing themselves that you're safe and serious about connecting, the dominant will next typically want to learn as much about what's in that naughty little noggin' of yours. Has your kink a specific costuming or role-play requirement? Do you need complicated sanitary specifications? Are you looking for more than one person to attend you?

There's also what toys and props the dominant has to provide, though most are also open to you bringing your own.

All of this is why it's essential to know exactly what you want before beginning your search. The more you understand your needs and can articulate them, the better the time you'll have.

So be open and honest with yourself, and equally as open and honest with your potential professional dominant. Try to keep in mind that, more than likely, this isn't the first time they've heard about the student who's come to their kindergarten teacher for an over-the-knee spanking.

It's crucial to remember that your professional dominant is that: a *professional*—and, as such, don't waste their time. Treat them with respect, and they'll do the same with you.

Now onto the etiquette of an actual session.

Basics out of the way first:

Show up. The number one complaint of escorts/doms, or anyone providing intimate services is *no-shows*.

Be on time. Depending on their mood, the dominant might not let you come in at all if you're more than a few minutes after your appointed time. Some might not let you reschedule if you disrespect their time. No excuses! Traffic be damned! Nothing will get you on the bad side of a professional faster than being rude or irresponsible. Rest assured, too, that your number and email address have been duly noted, so they'll know it's you despite you using a different name or trying to disguise your voice.

Also, keep in mind that if you *seriously* misbehave, you'll be blackballed–which is *not* a sexual term–from the community. As with the non-professional BDSM scene, professionals talk to one another and will quickly spread the word if you're unsafe or way too rude.

Showing your professional dominant that you respect their time and appreciate their services are the building blocks to a good session.

Paying for play

The second biggest complaint among professional dominants is *money*. They don't want clients haggling over prices or to be asked to provide something extra out of the goodness of their hearts. There are also some instances where they feel like they are simply not being paid enough.

In some circles, the money you surrender for a dominant's services is called a *tribute* or, in other cases, simply, *a gift*. Whatever the agreed-upon price for this tribute, remember, that's *the price*. No hemming or hawing!

Tips are accepted. They come at the end of your time. Your tribute should come before the session begins, unless you have made other arrangements.

Some doms prefer a card or envelope to hold the money. In contrast, others take credit cards or electronic payments before you show up. Don't be surprised if your dominant ask for a non-refundable deposit or small pre-payment. This way, if a client pulls a no show, they can at least collect a minimal fee for their time.

To make this easy on the dominant and yourself— set a price, keep to it, and pay them without complaint.

Now, onto the session…

The Session/Scene

Let's assume you've found the person of your dreams — yours, at least for an hour.

You've emailed a bit or talked once or twice (*briefly*, remember: they are not a phone sex service), you've met, you've bandied about your needs for the session and relinquished your tribute for their time—or have paid a small part of the fee to hold your time and book your session.

No matter what happens, don't try to change the game plan. Your dominant has fashioned your session to the specifications of what you've spoken about and agreed to, so don't think you can go switching horses by asking for something you never discussed. If you've come for a good old-fashioned over-the-knee spanking and then want diapering, don't demand it at the time but respectfully ask the dominant if they'd be game to try it during another session.

Be vocal if something isn't going to your liking. Dominants, by and large, aim to please. They want to create a safe yet wildly wicked atmosphere where clients can surrender control, release inhibitions, and find a blissful bottom headspace, and, of course, have their clients come back for more. While there are no guarantees, if you've found a well-respected professional dominant and communicated what you need and want—and what you *don't* want––then you're going to get what you pay for.

An excellent professional top can read a client, knowing when/how and where to throw in a little something that may be slightly to the left-of-center of your confessed need. They'll also learn how to pace things depending on how you're reacting, have safewords in place in case of emergencies, and will set aside a few minutes before the session so you can relax and get comfortable and a few minutes at the end for aftercare, if you need it.

This next issue is extremely important. It is probably the most significant complaint of professional dominants after payment issues or clients not showing up.

Here it is. Unless it's negotiated beforehand and can be legally performed, *your professional dominant will not have sex with you!*

Yes, a session can be sexual. You'll probably get a sexual/sensual/erotic quiver from the activities you engage in with your professional dominant, but visiting a dominant is not the same as seeing an escort.

Being allowed to orgasm at the end of your session can be negotiated, usually, not much more than masturbating—after the dominant grants permission, of course.

Arousal, too, is acceptable. Your dominant expects you to be turned on. But a scene is more about answering the mental need you have by engaging your body and mind in a specific way, with particular props and patter, with a Dominant dressed and accommodating that purpose, but *only that purpose* and nothing more.

Topping from the bottom

This depends on the dominant (top), as some don't mind polite and respectful guidance during the session while others will hand you your clothes and show you the door. You should be aware of what *topping from the bottom* means and why dominants aren't too keen on it.

Simply put, *topping from the bottom* is when a bottom, through word or deed, tries to run the session. You'd be surprised how many professional dominants complain about this aspect of the job. In many cases, they refuse a do session with anyone they sense will top from the bottom during the pre-screening phone call. Lots of people say they want to relinquish control, but what they actually want is to instruct the dominant how to smack them, what to say, when to do what they want, and so forth.

Now there is a big difference between asking for something and taking control away from a pro. Basically, it comes down to respect as well as mutual trust. If things aren't going the way you want, use your safeword and then directly communicate with the professional dominant and resist the urge to take control from them.

* * * *

Ideally, seeing a professional dominant should answer a need. You might want a professional to enact a fantasy, something you've thought about/masturbated over and has held you enraptured ever since your sexual awakening. Or maybe you want to connect with someone over your kink. A professional can address your needs and will understand and respect your desires without judgment.

CHAPTER 27:
What Did You Call Me?

Humiliation For Fun And Profit

As much as we've touched on lots of props and clothing in this kink section, you've probably noticed that a goodly amount of alternate sex play is about mental stimulation: roles played, imagined power exchanges, anticipation, the pricking of fantasy. (You can prick your fantasy, but can you fantasy your prick?) Into this mental stimulation comes another aspect of kink play that can be oh-so-fun and arousingly effective, *humiliation*.

What humiliation play may or may not look like depends on what the people involved have negotiated and mutually agreed-upon.

For example, it might involve what may at first glance appear to be verbal or physical abuse, like telling someone they're a "miserable little worm" or putting down their physical appearance or it could be nurturing such as saying a bottom is "such a lovely slut."

The fact is there are a nearly limitless number of different ways for someone to *consensually* humiliate another person—it's all a matter of being open and honest about what everyone wants, needs, and definitely doesn't want.

* * * *

When humiliation play involves deeply personal *exposure*, intentional or otherwise, it's recommended to play with utterly trustworthy people.

Not to make too much of a point of it, in this day and age, why the hell would you get intimate with anyone other than those you feel physically and emotionally safe with?

Delving into humiliation, either marrying it with something physical or on its own, respect for one another is imperative. You cannot, should not proceed without it.

In many cases, humiliation as a sexual turn-on hinges on playfully-demeaning certain aspects of the bottom's body or psyche. This can be extremely sensitive territory. Everyone has to tread very, very, *very* carefully, and then only if they know no matter what's said or done the people they're playing with will have their back.

Talking It Out

It's critical to view humiliation as immensely serious shit. When skirting the dark side of your bottom's soft white underbelly, please mark your words as well as your actions.

So how do you get to this point of respect and trust? How do you know what to say? How do you know what *not* to say?

The answer is relatively easy. *Talk to each other!*

Don't *ever* make any suppositions. In other words, don't *think* you know what is acceptable and what isn't. Rather you need to *know*, without question, and you learn this by having many in-depth conversations beforehand.

After that, make sure your lines of communication stay open and are clear as crystal. If it means dropping roles now and again then do it. Don't ever assume that things don't change, either over months and years, day-by-day, hour-by-hour, or minute-by-minute.

But what if you don't know your lover that well? Honestly, our advice is to stay away from humiliation play until you *do* have that kind of deep knowledge, as the potential for emotional abuse and injury is far too high.

Slow, backpedal, stop

In every kink scene, all *sexual* play actually, you must stay sharply aware of what's going on with your partner or playmate.

There you both are, getting hot and sweaty, blood pumping, senses reeling. Generally, both of you are deep in the heaving sea of arousal.

With humiliation, though, the top needs to be extra vigilant in keeping their eye and ear on what's going on, particularly as a bottom may not be able to clue you in to any sudden and unexpected onset of emotional trauma. You don't want to find out the hard way that someone is in distress.

If you hear *stop*, immediately do so. If you're the top and think you may have strayed too far from your own comfort zone, halt the action as well.

It doesn't have to be an all-or-nothing march to Nirvana here, as well. Sometimes everyone needs to slow down, do a little backpedaling, call a time-out to make sure things are going well. If not, or call the whole thing quits.

* * * *

We've all felt the brutal ache ourselves that can come from an unkind word, unjust criticism, feeling ignored, or plunged downward into seemingly unending depression from cruel mocking by a bully or emotional abuse from a parent.

Humiliation play can take on so many forms and can be wickedly arousing and fun. But never forget that when dealing with the fabric of someone's mind, you need to tread extremely carefully. While often injuries from physical play may heal in a short amount of time, those that wound us in our minds and souls can last a lifetime.

CHAPTER 28:
Hot and Drippy Is My Trippy

How to Have Fun (and Be Safe) With Wax Play

Amazingly intense, remarkably sensual, as soothing as a massage or as intense as a strike from a cane, wax play can be all of this and more. But, as it involves open flame and substances that burn there are some risks involved.

So here's a look at the glories as well as the potential drawbacks to having all kinds of kinky fun with a lit candle.

Fire

Safety should always (always, always, *always*) be first and foremost in your mind when engaging in any activity with an open flame. Literally, you're putting you and your playmate into a whole other realm when playing with fire.

Playspaces and private homes are often decorated or festooned with all manner of, well, *festoonery*: drapes, lace, papier-mâché decorations, cloth lampshades, and decorative tassels.

As you can rightly assume, none of these reacts well to fire. All it takes is a careless backhand and that lovely candle that gives your room that perfect ambiance tumbles to the floor, throwing un-fun and un-sexy wax all over the place and maybe setting the room ablaze.

So part one of flame safety is to make sure your environment is clean and uncluttered, beyond being mindful of the close proximity of decorations as well as any bedclothes, kerchiefs, tissues, silk scarves—you get the drift.

Part two is the most important: *have fire extinguishers handy!* One more time for the people in the back: *have fire extinguishers handy!*

When playing with flame, it should only be a table, a lighter, your candle, an extinguisher, and your playmate.

The Wax

It might sound trite, especially to something so critical, but not all candles are created equal.

Honestly, there's just one kind of candle you should use for wax play. Again, for the people in the back, *one kind of candle, only!*

They come in various names, though commonly they're referred to as safety candles (makes it easy, huh?). You can find them everywhere from pharmacies to hardware stores. They're simple and basic, you could even call them *dull*. But they are the *only* choice for this type of kinky play.

The thing about those other candles is that they often contain more than just wax, including colors, scents, or various chemicals—or, have an extremely high melting point.

For instance, soy wax candles typically soften at around 113-127 degrees (Fahrenheit), paraffin at 120 to 150 degrees, beeswax somewhere between 145 to 155, and gel wax also at nearly 145.

One thing you'll immediately notice about safety play candles is they're remarkably soft. All it takes is rubbing one between your fingers to get it melting, which is a very good thing. The softer the candle, the lower its melting point. With a low melting point, the hot wax landing on a person won't be excessively, painfully hot—and it cools down nicely fast.

There are even great kink entrepreneurs selling candles designed for wax play. Though even with these, always try out your candle on yourself (the back of the hand is a good place or your thigh if you're so inclined) before using it on someone else.

Do keep in mind, though, that everyone's pain threshold is different. Even if you think a particular heated wax feels acceptable for you, it might be too much for someone else.

So keep your lines of communication open. If the person you're dropping hot wax onto says that it's too hot for them, then, of course, listen! Then, react accordingly.

Hair

Another fun thing about hot wax is that with training, experience, and skill, it can be put practically anywhere. The keyword there is *practically*, as where you dribble and drop depends on how furry the person you're dropping wax on is. A bit of judicious shaving could be in order, extra if your playmate looks like a yeti.

On the subject of shaving, there's that *other* kind of wax play, the one so people use to get rid of hair. This can definitely be a kink. Though unless you're a professional, we don't recommend this for play as accidents can and has happened been the result of enthusiasm overriding actual expertise. This can lead to nasty burns or other irritation or damage to the skin.

If they happen to be reasonably hairless or recently trimmed or shaved, that doesn't mean you can dribble hot wax directly onto their bare skin.

Well, you *can*. But, applying a *small* amount of non-scented, nonflammable oil to your drippee's skin will make cleanup much easier. (Use non-scented oil because you don't want to add an unexpected allergic reaction to things you need to worry about.)

Baby oil or coconut oil works best here, though it's best to have your playmate bring their own so you won't have to try and guess what they like or don't.

Let's wax!

First: If your subject reacts negatively, along the lines of *Get this shit off me*, use your hand to smear the wax and immediately cool it down. Do not resist. Apply water or ice.

Distance from the candle's flame to the person you're playing with skin is crucial. Ideally, a scooch lower than a foot above your subject's skin is ideal. Any closer, and you risk the wax being too hot when it lands. Any farther away, it may splash all over the place.

Ideally, you want the candle to be parallel to your subject as well. If you tip the candle too far back, so the flame is above your hand, the wax is going to hit you and not them. Holding the candle directly down could cause the wax to catch fire and burn.

Move slowly and carefully over a small area, taking time to layer new wax over where you've already dribbled some. Wax play is the most intense where those first drops land, then easing off as layer after layer is built up, forming an insulating layer. This results in fostering a luxurious feeling of sensual warmth.

You can do your dribbling on the back, breasts, and nipples. All are fun zones, depending on personal preferences. Additionally, wax can be applied to someone's ass. It can be a vivid experience especially before, during, or after impact play. And can be explored, with extra, extra, *extra* precautions, on genitalia.

On a side note, breasts (with the person lying down) can be fun as the wax can make a lovely mold of that person's nipple, giving them a sexy souvenir to take home.

Stay away from anything above a person's neck. (*Duh!*)

Slowly and sensually, you've laid a growing area of wax on your bottom. They're feeling the warmth and the lovely intensity, but now it's time to come back to reality.

And here's where we get to the *messy* part.

Cleanup

Due to how much of a pain it can be to clean up after, most kink play spaces do not allow wax play. Ask the owner or Dungeon Monitor before getting out your candle and lighter.

At home, place an old sheet you're never going to use again under the person you're going to wax. This way, when the scene is over, gently brush the wax off of them and throw the sheet away. Suffice it to say, if there's a rug or any kind of carpeting nearby, up your carefulness as removing wax out of either can be a nightmare.

Just like how we find sand in the most unusual body crevices after a trip to the beach, after wax play the bottom will discover wax in places you didn't even drip. Moreso if your bottom enjoys it to the point where they're flipping around you dribble on them. Luckily, when wax dries (at least on skin sans hair), it's easy to pluck off.

There are also kink games involving the top cleaning the wax from their bottom by whipping the wax off them. If you try this, it makes cleanup especially hard as the wax will fly everywhere.

* * * *

So go forth and heat up your life with hot wax. Just remember that you're dealing with fire and a substance that will *burn* if not properly tested or controlled. If you have any doubts, light that other candle, the one of knowledge by reading, taking classes, or consulting an expert.

CHAPTER 29:
Oh No You Don't

The Intricacies of Chastity

Of the kinks we've covered here, chastity seems to be definitely on the rise. As for why, maybe it's because we're living in a society too often based on immediate satiation, so the idea of being denied, tempered, or teased is a refreshing novelty.

Chastity is defined by Miriam Webster as: "the quality or state of being chaste." (Thanks for that, didn't anyone ever tell you not to define a word by using the word in the definition? Jeez!) They add, "abstention from all sexual intercourse."

There are tons of ways to do this, from a top telling a bottom to keep their hands to themselves—to physical restraints, but whatever the means, the result can be an extremely potent erotic tool.

Even so, anyone interested in chastity needs to be aware of the many intricacies and possible risks that might arise when trying this intensely arousing power play dynamic.

To begin with, as we've said more than once, the *idea* of a thing can be way different from the actual *doing* of a thing. A top and/or bottom fantasizing that denying orgasm is the most wonderful sexual play ever invented, then discovering that no matter how hot the idea might appear to be in practice, it simply doesn't work for them.

For a bottom, denial may negatively affect their psyche, even for a short amount of time. Sure, this *is* the point of this chastity stuff after all, but that doesn't excuse those involved from turning a blind eye to the difference between BDSM fun and anguish, the real thing.

People who are not familiar with each other should not delve into these types of play until everyone can discern when things *have* crossed that line. In the beginning, it's probably wise to limit the duration and intensity of chastity play.

And, no, we're not being unnecessarily cautious. Everything from having a momentary emotional crisis to long-lasting psychological challenges, including profound depression, can and have occurred as the result of ill-thought-out or enacted chastity play.

Tops must stay in constant contact with their bottom, particularly in cases where they may not be able to quickly signal if they're in trouble. Conversely, the bottom should speak up if experiencing more than they bargained for.

It's also vital that tops keep their own needs and desires in check. Tops cannot let their pride or inability to admit a scene isn't working interfere with their responsibility to the bottom. If a top fucked up in some way, they too can call their safeword.

These cautions are true for partners even if merely dabbling with chastity. Everyone should be aware of what's going on physically as well as mentally in regards to chastity devices or denying someone's sexual release.

Aside from emotional concerns, they're practical things to consider.

For instance, if someone is kept in a device with an *actual* lock, make sure you know where you keep that damned key!

Classic naughty pictures show a chastity cage key dangling between someone's hefty cleavage or on a chain around a comely ankle. Keep in mind that these keys can fall off their chains, get misplaced, bend or break, so have a spare one handy at all times—or just in case, a pair of bolt cutters. Hygiene can also be a concern. The good news is that chastity devices, like all modern-day sex toys, are constructed of materials that are as tough as they are hypoallergenic. These toys are constructed so the wearer can urinate and clean themselves easily.

For penis-equipped, there are conflicting schools of thought on what is healthy and what not when it comes to being kept from ejaculating and keeping said penis caged/having one's erections halted mid-unfurl.

The jury's still out on any long-term effects on cocks in cages, though there are reams and reams of pages across the internet from those who've had no ill effects from long-term internment. Thought, as we suggest with so many things in this book, *proceed with caution.*

Pain in the plumbing is an indicator that something might be wrong. Equally, be aware that many dire consequences won't be felt or seen until the penis has been released from confinement.

Chastity for the vagina-equipped has its own set of challenges. The most obvious is that while the famed chastity belt for the vagina-equipped may prevent penetration or clitoral stimulation, some people can still orgasm with minimal physical contact or via nipple stimulation (lucky you!).

In response to this, a skilled top might need to adjust their commands or use specialized gear to keep someone in chastity.

Sometimes chastity involves more of an honor-system set-up than a physical one.

Hardware

Taking into account how much of your sex life you want to make public, you will want a device that can be worn while out-and-about *or* gotten into and out of quickly and carefully.

Like with bondage gear, chastity hardware should be selected for comfort and ease-of-maintenance and *never* for affordability. You don't want a cheap piece of equipment giving your bottom a nasty infection or an injury that might affect their sexual health for the rest of their lives!

To avoid this, buy from dealers who know what they're doing. Seek out experts in chastity and not amateur enthusiasts. You also must be prepared to go through a trial and error phase. You may have to buy and try several devices to find what works and ditch the ones that don't.

You can reduce the inconvenience of this phase by asking people who have years under their (*ahem*) chastity belts. Specifically, ask about their drawers and drawers of devices that they paid good money for and ending up discarding.

In addition to talking to others, don't forget to talk to your partner as one does in all kink. If something doesn't feel right, for any reason, the restrained should be released immediately.

So don't buy a new piece of gear, slap your bottom into it, and then send them home for the weekend. Instead, put them into it and see how they feel for half an hour, two hours, then four, then a day. Always grant them a way to get out of it by themselves, emotionally as well as physically, if anything goes wrong.

Some more notes on going out in public: the internet is riddled with stories of people walking through airport detectors, either informing the security agents that they were wearing a specific piece of jewelry or a prosthetic as the scanners go off. There have also been occasions when a same-gender TSA agent has taken someone off to a room to make a more thorough inspection. That said, chastity fans report that many TSA agents have *seen this a hundred times*. It's more likely you're going to freak out old Aunt Bessie than anyone at airport security. Still, it's recommended to take off your device before getting on the plane and replace it when you reach your destination.

* * * *

Chastity can be a constant reminder of consensually giving control of one's body to another person. In some cases, the bottom becomes a cuckold kept under lock and key while their lover goes out and plays. For others, it's an exciting addition to their regular bedroom antics.

No matter the degree, everyone needs to consider the arrangement. The actual physical *nuts and bolts* of this kink/lifestyle/diversion is the most elementary part. While mental anguish from denial, married with physical discomfort, might be what this kink is about for some, everyone involved needs to be constantly aware of what's happening. Be prepared to grant sexual freedom, and emotional comfort, when necessary.

CHAPTER 30:
Cupping the light fantastic

The Art Of Cupping

Though not as intense as other BDSM activities, there's a lot to be said for the sensation of warmth, weight, and the gentle suction that comes from cupping, especially as a relaxing warm-up to a scene or as soothing aftercare conclusion.

It's a matter of debate about which country or even region first developed cupping. Some like to give China credit, while others feel strongly that it started in the Middle East. Most, however, agree that it's incredibly ancient. Evidence suggesting the appearance of cupping in the teachings of Muhammad and as far back as on ancient Egyptian papyrus scrolls. A conservative estimate of cupping's origins go as far back as (drum roll please) 3,000 years ago.

There are three methods of cupping: dry cupping, fire cupping, and wet cupping. Dry cupping creates a partial vacuum through mechanical means. Fire cupping is the same but with (obviously) fire. Wet cupping is either of the first two methods while adding minor lacerations to the cupping recipient's back, so the suction pulls out small amounts of blood.

Dry cupping is spectacularly easy and remarkably safe. And though there are all kinds of ancient means to do this kind of suction, it's recommended to engage modern ways. As for how to acquire a dry cupping set, welcome to the 21st century. A quick Amazon search for "dry cupping set" will net you dozens of options, all around the 20 to 60 dollar range.

Though some use silicone, the plastic bell-type seems to be all the rage as they usually come in a wide variety of shapes and sizes of cups, plus a nifty little vacuum pump to do the *sucking*. We suggest this type as the silicone kind has an "on or off" degree of suction, as opposed to the mechanical pump with their typically three or so levels of intensity and a built-in limiter that keeps the suction from getting too intense.

A key advantage to dry cupping is its reliability of suction and durability. With any of these mechanical sets, anyone can apply cups to about every part of the body (more on this in a bit) with enough force that they won't spontaneously pop off.

Agreed, you won't have the warmth and weight that glass cups heated with fire provides, but if one of those plastic cups comes free, it won't shatter into a million razor-sharp bits when it hits the floor. Because of this, it's rarely a good idea to do anything but dry cupping in a dungeon.

Fire cupping, though, is often more sensual and relaxing or stimulating if used at the start of a scene to warm up the person who's about to be canned, spanked, flogged, and such-like. As we said, glass cups are heavy-ish, and their suction-power isn't as predictable as a dry cupping set, though they usually have more than enough suction to get the job done. Their glass construction additionally conducts a nice amount of heat, making them deliciously warm when applied.

As for where to get glass cups, back to Amazon. Though note that they can be a wee bit pricy—not because of the glass cups themselves, which are relatively cheap (around $3 a cup) but due to the cost of shipping heavy, glass objects. If you're lucky enough to live in an area with a large Asian community, you may find glass cups in shops carrying herbs and acupuncture supplies.

Light me up!

Sadly, and too frequently *tragically*, there's a lot of misinformation floating around about fire cupping.

As with anything in BDSM, read, read, *read.* Watch videos over and over and over again. Take class after class after class before trying anything, especially anything involving open flame.

Part of this misinformation lies in not understanding the principle of fire cupping. Without getting all *Mr. Wizard* on you (look him up if you don't know who Mr. Wizard is), the goal is to raise the temperature *inside* the cup and *not* the glass.

Let's repeat that last bit, shall we:

R*aise the temperature* inside *the cup and* not *the glass* so that after you place the cup on the skin and the air inside the cup cools, it'll produce a partial vacuum, and thus suction.

If you allow the flame to linger on the inside of the cup too long, potentially dangerously high levels of heat will spread throughout the glass resulting in burning the person being cupped.

There's really one—*only* one—safe and effective way to heat the air in a glass cup.

Yet again, let's drum this into your brains.

Repeat this last bit, shall we:

*There's really one—*only one*—safe and effective way to heat the air in a glass cup!*

We're so sure about this, based on cups and cups and cups of experience with cupping, we have no problem (at all) saying that if any other way is flat-out wrong! Worse still, they have an excellent chance of causing severe injury.

These wrong ways include things like pouring alcohol into a glass cup, igniting it and placing it on some poor unfortunate person's back, rubbing an alcohol-soaked and lit cotton ball on the inside of a cup, and using a candle to do the heating. Or for the worst one—and you can wince along with us—a blow torch.

That is hopefully out of the way.

Here's how to properly heat up a glass cup: take a stick (or camping) lighter, click it on, wave it inside the cup. Again, avoiding hitting the actual glass. Then, *immediately* put the cup on your person.

That's it.

That's the only good, safe way to do glass cupping.

By the way, we suggest the camp lighter as opposed to something like a candle or regular lighter. With the former, it's too hard to keep the flame away from the glass. It can also wreck your wrist getting it into the cup where it can heat the air inside.

To get a fair approximation of what a glass cup feels like, and always before applying one to someone else, test drive it by using your own thigh. If it's too hot, you're either leaving the flame in the cup too long or you are heating the glass.

Also, keep in mind that the more you use a cup, the warmer it will get. Thus, its suction becomes less and less intense. To keep the cups cool-*ish*, you could apply a tiny amount of lukewarm, though not cold, water on them. If they are too chilled, there's more of a possible chance that they'll crack or shatter.

As with a lot of fun naughty activities, lubrication when glass cupping is essential. Though dry cups will stick without anything applied to a person's skin, they'll do a superior job after applying a small amount of oil, to the person and not the cups, obviously.

For fire cupping, as for wax play, it's just about essential to employ some kind of oil. Coconut or baby oil, or anything akin to them works well. Keep the amount you use minimal, and keep any open flame far, far away!

Blood and glass

Wet cupping?

Hate to disappoint, but you're not going to learn about it from us.

Why? Well, to begin with, we don't have as much experience with mixing cutting with dry or fire cupping and so can't really advise you about it.

More importantly, as it involves blood, the stakes involved go through the roof. As such, we don't feel comfortable suggesting it for anyone except well-seasoned BDSM practitioners. Even then, proceed with a great deal of caution. As with anything involving bodily fluids, participants should know EXACTLY what they're doing, including how to prepare for the scene. Everything must be cleaned and sterilized beforehand. Participants must know the kind and location of cuts to make and what instruments to use. After play, instruments and wounds must be cleaned and sterilized. Plus, people must be aware of every blood-borne pathogen, illnesses, or health-related condition. And perhaps most importantly, those in the scene must know what do to do the *instant* anything goes wrong.

Where to cup

With dry cupping, pretty much anywhere on the body is fair game. Most commonly, they're placed on the back, though they can additionally be used for tit or genital play. Be cautious about the amount of suction on these sensitive bits.

Once again: read, read, read, watch, watch, watch, study, study, study before you try something like that.

With fire cupping, the back is the place for play. This is because if you place a cup on someone who is standing, the weight of the glass will pop it off, and like we said, suddenly you have a billion glass shards on the floor.

If someone lays on their back, breasts and chests can also shift and move quite a bit, making a good seal challenging to achieve. Face down, pop-offs can still happen. Don't depend on your less-than-lighting-fast reflexes to catch them. Instead, make sure there's a safe zone on the floor and all around you.

Regarding how long to leave them on, a good measure is to test on your cupping subject. Then, after communication, slowly increasing the number and duration. There are those that as few as five minutes and as long as 45, though this might be a bit much for beginners.

* * * *

We love to teach cupping because, except for the wet variety, it can be a wonderfully safe activity. The only thing to worry about is your subject looking like they've been attacked by a rather amorous octopus, but otherwise, they'll be fine.

And though cupping may not be one of the wildest of activities, it can be a lovely meditative experience, a fantastic relaxation technique, curative (on its own or with acupuncture), or excellent warm-up or aftercare for BDSM scenes as well as life in general.

CHAPTER 31:
Interview: Chris and Ralph by Chris and Ralph

The only unnatural sex act is that which you cannot perform.
—ALFRED KINSEY

What follows are some questions I asked Chris and his answers. [*Then my questions to Ralph*]. You'll find a theme here. We didn't want to go all willy-nilly [*Are you Willy or am I Nilly or is it the other way around?*] asking each other a whole bunch of stuff that might have meandered, loquacious as we have been known to be.

As with all the other professionals we interview herein, we figured why not get some nuggets from the old horses' mouths [*Wilbur!*]. Not that we haven't had our say throughout this book, but it's fun when we get to ask each other stuff, be all serious and sheet [*Yes, the very few times that happens*].

So here we go with the meaty Chris and Ralph interview.

* * * *

Ralph asks Chris:

Q. What do you think of the state of sexuality in the modern world? Are we doomed, on the precipice of great extraordinary changes, or is it the same old same old, and I am just mistaken (as I often am)?

A. I don't think you're mistaken … far from it! I'm not sure about you, but I often feel like I'm caught between two worlds. According to the most awful invention in the history of history, the calendar, I'm, well, let's call it well-seasoned.

Emotionally, philosophically, though I'm closer to members of the so-called Millennial generation — notably when it comes to sex — with much of it stemming from a lifetime of devouring science fiction, so a predisposition to question pre-conceptions and a willingness to embrace change.

There's a kind of erotic thrill to see how things are progressing. Despite (as I write this in 2024) having had a racist in the White House, we're seeing the growing acceptance of LGBT+ sexuality and gender fluidity, the essential necessity of consent, the right to be free from sexual harassment and violence, the spreading recognition of everything from BDSM sex to polyam, and so much more.

That tipped my hand a bit. Yeah, I *do* think things are getting better. There are some rough spots, like trying to kick toxic masculinity to the curb and a still-persistent attitude that sex is to be given or taken instead of shared. Despite this, I feel we're heading in the right direction.

Besides, if we embrace fear, then all that will happen is we'll become more and more frustrated, if not terrified, of progress. So it's much better to keep both eyes open, think logically and compassionately, and resist falling victim to it's all been downhill from the mythical the good old days.

As I said before, I've lived those days (and years) and am damned eager to leave that ignorance and hate far behind.

For some, the future might be strange or even frightening or but it's coming whether they want it to or not, so (IMHO) it's wiser to dream, and strive towards, a tomorrow that's happier, healthier, thoughtful, conscientious, caring, and *passionate* than tomorrow ever was.

Q. In our speaking/teaching engagements, what interests you most (other than how wonderful it is to spend time with yours truly).

A. I'm not sure I understand the question: you mean there's *another* reason to go to events aside from spending time with my BFF? Okay, it's that we get to see how diverse and cool the sexual and kink communities are!

That and we get to play tourist. Win-win!

Q. In the many years you were active in the San Francisco 'scene' (and I know you're not so active in that scene personally these days, but you still teach/work in kink). What seems to have changed the most? What do you wish was still around?

A. Well, I'm still *somewhat* in the BDSM scene, though no longer as much as I was and not in the Bay Area having left it behind for Eugene, Oregon two years ago.

I got into kink back in '88, when dinosaurs ruled the earth and the Internet was nothing but the fever dreams of geeks. I had a great time, but, like a lot of people, it took me quite some time to find out who I was and am.

After a decade or two away from the scene, I came back with a renewed passion, jumping into teaching classes, running support groups, and stuff-like-that-there.

I've never been nostalgic, though I have noticed how the BDSM community has changed over the years. The biggest, and perhaps the most depressing, is the fall of San Francisco from a place where people can live to a cold-hearted bastion of everything wrong with capitalism.

To put it another way, just as I did in 2019, many Bay Area kinksters left because they couldn't afford to stay.

The other thing I've noticed is that there used to be a lovely system of progression in the BDSM community back then. You'd join a public group, like the Society Of Janus, and, after spending time there, you gained friends and connections/doors would open leading to all kinds of relationships, events, and party opportunities. The scene also had a very hands-on mentoring system where newbies learned what they needed to know, taught by experts and the community itself.

Q. What are we missing most these days in intimate interaction?

I think it's less what we're missing and more about how we are changing. Before the Interwebs, it was tough to educate yourself, especially when it came to sex. Now you can learn practically all you ever needed to know about every aspect of human sexuality on your smartphone while staying in immediate contact with nearly everyone on the planet at the same time.

Then there's that no matter who you are or who you love, with minimal effort, you can find your tribe or merely discover you aren't alone. There are innumerable people who feel and desire the same.

If we work hard and play our cards right, our contemporary growing pains might someday lead to the end of sexual ignorance, intolerance, violence, and most of all, *loneliness.*

Chris asks Ralph

Q. Are we undergoing a new sexual revolution?

A.New? I doubt it. There's nothing happening now that hasn't happened before. The ole nothing new under the sun axiom. We might be seeing and hearing about more stuff nowadays because people have access (and a sad need) to reveal more of their personal business to the masses than they ever have had before.

Maybe a few newer kinks have come about via the net and technology. I'm thinking VR/MR/AI here or some better sex toys. But no, I don't think we are undergoing a sexual revolution. Though, as you well know, lots of people want to think we are so they can feel that much better about themselves and mankind presently. Or at least tweet about it.

Q. What are some of the biggest things you've personally discovered about sex?

A. That it's fun? Well, even before I was sexual, I always suspected that it would be fun. Maybe as I grow older, the one thing I have come to realize most is that all sexual/intimate expression is wonderful, from kissing to nipple touching to anything else. I don't seem to hold a "First base" "Second base" idea of sex these days, if I ever really did. It is all part of just that wonderful and wacky world of being human.

Q. Do you sometimes feel, like I do, that we're straddling the old world of sex and the new?

Certainly with the infiltration of technology, yes, I feel that way, as I said before. But in the face of that technology, that old and new, I feel the human-animal really hasn't made all the much progress. To me, that's the more important point. In many ways, I often think of the band Devo's stance: I take a look around and feel more often than not that we are de-evolving.

I think the new world, in almost every way, has us reacting (not you and I, of course, being two of the most highly evolved and fantastically cultured beings on the planet) as fantastically stressed Dodo birds, walking around with our heads firmly plastered up our keisters in lieu of real interaction.

But then again, I could be wrong.

Q. If you could tell your younger self anything about sex, what would it be?

A. Slow the fuck down, Ralphie! Savor every moment (not just in sexual situations) and try and get as much as you can on video (it was video way back then, before that, Polaroids.) Although I do tend to hate the damn machine, what I wouldn't have given for my cell phone's video and picture capabilities back in the day.

Q. What's the most surprising thing you've come across in the kinky world?

A. Not that I hadn't suspected this, but as we say all the time, kinky folk are all so normal, and outright welcoming. That might come as a surprise, I know to those people who don't court a kink or think we are all perverts. But as we travel across the country teaching our classes or in the correspondence I manage with interviewing people in the business or just hanging around kinksters in general, I'd say give me the pervert, the fetishist, the kinkster anytime over anybody else!

Q. One thing about this crazy new world is that there seem to be so many fantastic sexual subcultures. Do you feel they are a new thing, or have they always been there but almost invisible?

A. No, there is nothing new under the sun. We might call it something totally different or want to kid ourselves we are so evolved that whatever we are into or whatever we call ourselves has to be a thing wholly of our times. But no, none of the stuff we see today, on Clips4sale downloads, to what we might try in our bedroom to those multitude of labels we give ourselves is so radically different than anything that has gone before. Maybe we hid our desires and self-definitions from society in the past all that much more because we knew they wouldn't be so readily accepted. But really I think there were always sexual subcultures and even places where the like-minded met to commiserate as much as copulate.

OUR GLORIOUS GLOSSARY OF SEX TERMINOLOGY

Just so we're all on the same page with this book (get it? on the same page?), we figured we'd include with a brief glossary.

Emphasis on the *brief* part, as a totally comprehensive one would be longer than this magnificent (if we do so say so ourselves) tome. So let's assume when we use *anal* we don't mean "They're a bit of a stickler."

Some of the below are simply briefer definitions on what we've expounded on and explored further in the book. Sorry if we're repeating ourselves, but at least you'll get some pithy definitions here if you've chosen to skip over whole chapters where the word might be defined at length.

So here goes nuffin'...

Age play (BDSM): Any sexual activity/kink play/lifestyle where one or more partners act or pretend to be a different age (usually younger) through speech, dress, and mannerisms. This is strictly, and always *adult* kink behavior, it should never, ever, EVER involve actual children.

Anilingus: Mouth-to-anus stimulation

Anthropomorphic: To have a human form. 'Furries' often refer to their animal alter-egos as being anthropomorphic. What's a furry you ask, well...

AR: Augmented reality, similar to virtual reality (VR) except that images are superimposed over the real world.

BDSM: Though this acronym could easily stand for *Big Dogs Smell Musty* for our purposes, it's the abbreviation for Bondage/Discipline/Sadism/Masochism.

Bigs (BDSM): (also *Daddys* or *Mommys*) a person who is the caretaker, the individual playing dominant or parent in the infantilism sexual activity/kink play/lifestyle. See also: Infantilism, and Age Play.

Bisexuality: Sexual desire for a genders xxx. The term *heteroflexible* has come into present parlance and for many means is synonymous with bisexuality. Best to ask first before whipping whatever it is you have, out.

Bondage (BDSM): Any sexual activity/kink play/lifestyle where one purposely restricts another or one restricts their own movements. Shibari rope play, mummification, even chastity, and much more, could all be considered a form of bondage.

Bottom (BDSM): The person receiving punishments, instruction, being humiliated or ordered; the one 'submitting' to the desires of their top. See also

Bukkake: slang. Japanese term for ejaculating onto a person's body or face.

Chode: slang. A fat, thick, penis.

Cornhole: slang. Anal sex.

Cosplay: Dressing up as a character who is defined by their costume, the props they use and the fantasy world they occupy in culture; i.e., video game characters, comic superheroes or villains.

Cross-dressing: Someone who finds either comfort or sexual arousal by dressing in the clothes of a different gender.

Cuckolding and Cuckqueaning (BDSM): The fetish (some would call it a lifestyle) where a male-identified person in a relationship is aware of and often does indeed encourage their partner taking other sexual partners. Cuckqueaning is when a female-identified person in a relationship wants their partner to have sex with other partners.

Cunnilingus: Mouth-to-vagina stimulation. Yum.

Cupping: Sensual and also medicinal use of cups (usually glass) to create a partial vacuum against the skin.

DM (BDSM): Abbreviation for the term *Dungeon Monitor*, (or "Doodie Markle" great star of stage and silver screen, known for their masterful rendition of "The Saints, They Aint A'Marchin Anywhere, Despite What You've Heard To The Contrary") responsible for the protocols, playing and overall safety and decorum of the dungeon they policies.

Emerophilia: Fetish involving vomit also called a *Roman Shower* (slang).

Exhibitionism: Any sexual activity/kink play/lifestyle that is based on the desire to expose oneself, or another, in public. Or, the reason why your neighbors have been keeping their blinds open since you moved in; they've heard about what you're into and are into it too!

Blowjob: Mouth-to-penis stimulation. More yum.

Femdom (BDSM): A female-identified person who is the top during a BDSM play scene, or the term to describe those activities.

Fetish (BDSM): Intense sexual desire for an object, body part or article of clothing.

Fetlife (BDSM): A free website popular with aficionados of kink and BDSM (www.fetlife.com).

Furries: slang. Though often without a sexual component, for our purposes people deriving a sexual thrill from dressing as an animal.

Golden shower: slang. Sexual play involving urine.

Homosexuality: Sexual desire for the same gender.

Impact play (BDSM) : Any sexual activity/kink play/lifestyle where one person either strikes another or themselves.

Kink (BDSM): Intense sexual desire for a specific activity.

Masturbation: Sexual self-pleasure. *See also*: nothing wrong with.

Ménage à trios: Three people engaged in a sex activity (oh, you lucky bugger you!)

Monogamy: The practice of having sex, being intimate, with only one partner at a time.

OTK (BDSM): Abbreviation for the classic Over-The-Knee a position a spankee might find themselves in lying across the lap of their spanker.

Pearl necklace: slang. To ejaculate on a person's upper chest or neck.

Pegging (BDSM): slang. Often used to describe someone wearing a dildo, (or holding one) to engage in anal sex with a partner.

Phthalates: chemicals added to materials (mostly PVC plastics) that would increase the plastic's flexibility and durability. Generally not used any longer in modern day adult toy making as phthalates were found to be harmful to the environment and to humans (that damn environment always gets the first consideration).

Polyamory: "The practice of, or desire for, intimate relationships with more than one partner, with the knowledge of all partners." (thank you, Wikipedia)

Queening: slang. The act of a female-identified person sitting on someone's face, usually in a femdom context.

Roleplay (BDSM): Any sexual activity/kink play/lifestyle where one or more partners act/pretend a 'role'–through speech, dress, mannerisms, supposed concerns–that they are not.

Safeword (BDSM): A word or phrase, that spoken by a Bottom/Submissive causes all sexual or kink action being perpetrated by a top to stop.

Scat (BDSM): slang. Sexual play involving feces.

Sexting: To send, sometimes explicit, or just flirty, texts, video posts, pictures and messages from one cell phone to another.

Teabagging: slang. When testicles slap the face of another person. Also, a dick move in video games.

Top (BDSM): The top in the relationship. This person orders, doles out punishment and pleasure; basically, the person who controls the submissive *(see: Bottom/Submissive)*

Topping from below (BDSM): Term used in a kink scene when a Submissive/Bottom directs, either by word or deed, the play, influencing a top into doing what they, the bottom wants.

Tranny: derogatory (and frankly insulting, your mother brought you up better than that!) Term for a transgender individual or someone who engages in cross-dressing.

Transgender: people having a gender identity or gender expression that differs from their assigned sex.

Unicorns: That majestic fantasy creature which comes galloping to your side as you cast your magical wonderfulness on the wind. For our purposes here, the word defines a single female that a straight couple sexually seeks.

Voyeurism: A sexual activity/kink play/lifestyle based on looking at others engaging in some sort of sexual activity. Or, the reason why your neighbors have been keeping their blinds *closed* since you moved in; they've heard about what you're into and think you're a sicko!

VR–Virtual Reality: the use of technology, such as video-goggles, to block out real reality and instead view an artificial (virtual) one.

RESOURCES

Answer: a wonderful source of sexual education, sponsored by Rutgers University. http://answer.rutgers.edu.

Planned Parenthood: the definitive place for sexual health and information. www.plannedparenthood.org.

Respect Ability: a fantastic site run by and for those with disabilities focusing on sexual issues and concerns. www.respectability.org

San Francisco Sex Information (SFSI): a non-judgmental, non-profit, comprehensive sex information organization. sfsi.org. (415) 989-SFSI (7374).

AFTERWARD:
The Morning After

Sexually progressive cultures gave us literature, philosophy,
civilization and the rest, while sexually restrictive cultures gave us
the Dark Ages and the Holocaust.
—ALAN MOORE, *25,000 YEARS OF EROTIC FREEDOM*

Congratulations, you have successfully completed reading our book, and if you haven't, and you just skipped to the back, then what in the *hell* is wrong with you? I mean, seriously! I've seen some sick shit in my days — don't get me started about that time with the un-ripened kumquat and the linoleum panties–but to read the afterward before the forward, that's just fucking *wrong*.

But if you've read the entirety of our little sexual education book, then we sincerely hope you've enjoyed it. In thanks, we'd like to send you a complimentary t-shirt that you can proudly wear and display your momentous accomplishment.

Note: offer not valid on Earth or any other outlying planetary bodies.

By now you may be feeling one of two things: (a) total confusion and absolute intimidation, stemming from an overload of raw sexual information as well as having your head blown by this new and beautiful (no, that's not sarcasm) world of consent, responsibility, empathy, tolerance, and acceptance; and (b) a monumental yawn coming on as we have not covered, or not covered enough, the depths of your glorious depravity. If the latter, then I have a pair of size six linoleum panties you might be interested in (the fruit, alas, has spoiled).

Kidding aside, we know this is a bit much to absorb, and may feel like sex, and what it all can mean these days, has changed too much too fast. Rest assured, though, that, at its core (it's juicy, squishy, sweaty, tasty core) sex hasn't changed at all.

Understanding and most of all *practicing* consent, responsibility, empathy, tolerance, and acceptance doesn't make sex any less hot, though hopefully it'll make it far less emotionally and physically painful now and in the years to come.

Too complex?

What if I put it this way— as long as everyone involved knows and accepts the risks involved, consents (and understands that it can and must be an ongoing process with no repercussions if rescinded), takes responsibility should things go wrong, embraces conscientiousness and empathy, views sex as something to be shared, then go forth and *play*.

There's always so much more to learn. So get out there and try new things. See what works (or doesn't … and don't worry, not everything will). Experiment, indulge and, most of all, have fun!

–M.Christian, 2024

ABOUT THE AUTHORS

While both Ralph and Chris love to write, they also both enjoy teaching. Whether it's about the exciting world of erotica story-telling or delving into any of the sexual subjects here in this book, they always bring a lot of energy, sensitivity, and bust-a-gut humor to each class.

Be sure and check out what they teach and when on their mutual site at www.rgreco-and-mchristian-presents.com and listen in on their fabulous (we we do say so ourselves) *Licking Non-Vanilla* podcast: www.lickingnonvanilla.com.

* * * *

Calling **M.Christian** versatile is a tremendous understatement. Extensively published in science fiction, fantasy, horror, thrillers, and even nonfiction, it is in erotica that M.Christian has become an acknowledged master, with stories in such anthologies as *Best American Erotica, Best Gay Erotica, Best Lesbian Erotica, Best Bisexual Erotica, Best Fetish Erotica*, and in fact too many anthologies, magazines, and sites to name.

In erotica, M.Christian is known and respected not just for their passion on the page but also their staggering imagination and chameleonic ability to successfully and convincingly write for any and all orientations.

But M.Christian has other tricks up their literary sleeve. In addition to writing, they are a prolific and respected anthologist, having edited twenty-five anthologies to date, including the *Best S/M Erotica* series; *Pirate Booty; My Love For All That Is Bizarre: Sherlock Holmes Erotica; The Burning Pen; The Mammoth Book of Future Cops* and *The Mammoth Book of Tales of the Road* (with Maxim Jakubowksi); *Confessions, Garden of Perverse, Amazons* (with Sage Vivant), and many more.

M.Christian's short fiction has been collected in many bestselling books in a wide variety of genres, including the Lambda Award finalist *Dirty Words* and other queer collections like *Filthy Boys* and *BodyWork*, as well as BDSM focused books like *In Control: The Short, Kinky, Otherworldly Fiction Of M.Christian* out now from Parisian Phoenix Publishing.

They also have published collections of nonfiction (*Welcome to Weirdsville, Pornotopia*, and *How to Write and Sell Erotica*); science fiction, fantasy, and horror *(Love Without Gun Control)*; and erotic science fiction including *Rude Mechanics, Technorotica, Better Than the Real Thing*, the acclaimed *The Bachelor*

Machine, Skin Effect, and *Hard Drive.* As a novelist, M.Christian has shown their monumental versatility with books such as the queer vamp novels *Running Dry* and *The Very Bloody Marys*; the erotic romance *Brushes (available in 2025 as special new addition from Parisian Phoenix Publishing)* ; the science fiction erotic novel *Painted Doll;* and the rather controversial gay horror/thrillers *Finger's Breadth* and *Me2*.

M.Christian has also become a celebrated sexual futurist, both through their novels and short stories as well as being a Managing Editor/Senior Columnist for *Future Of Sex*, which provides "insights into the fascinating topic of the future of human sex and sexuality."

Their site is www.mchristian.com.

Ralph Greco, Jr. is the devilishly clever pseudonym for Ralph Greco, an internationally published author of interviews and reviews, essays, scripts, webcopy, and articles, fiction, songs and one-act plays. Ralph is the editor of www.AIPDaily.com, a semi-regular contributor to www.sexpert.com, *Darkside Magazine, Kink Queens Magazine*, and the senior east coast correspondent at www.vintagerock.com. Ralph's short fiction collections have been published by Renaissance eBooks, Wordwooze and Pink Flamingo...and with the wonderful publisher of this book, and quite a few other titles by Ralph, Parisian Phoenix. His non-fiction has appeared in national magazine as diverse as *PROG, Nature, Newsweek* and *HUSTLER*.

Along with M. Christian, Ralph is the co-host of the Licking Non-Vanilla podcast, which was built from the dynamic duo teaching classes at kink conventions across the U.S. His music can be found at (again, at the so cleverly named) www.ralphgrecomusic.com.

When Mr. Greco has the time he also attempts to keep his ever-expanding ego from running amok in the wild environs of Northern New Jersey suburbia.

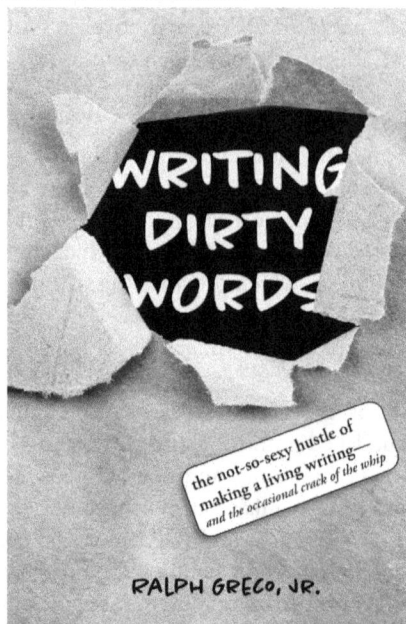

PARISIAN PHOENIX PUBLISHING KINK PRESENTS

WRITING DIRTY WORDS
The not-so-sexy hustle of making a living writing
(and the occasional crack of the whip)

Writing Dirty Words presents a witty, easy going romp through a full-time, freelance 'literary' career—useful as tips for the aspiring income-earning writer (or anybody attempting to create anything, really) and as a memoir of musician, playwright, children's book writer and erotica author Ralph Greco, Jr. Inside these pages, Ralph shares his personal anecdotes about how and for whom he built his writing career which just so happened to focus on erotica. He didn't intend to write naughty stories, but he did what any hungry writer does; he pursued the opportunities that crossed his path and built on what developed. This is the ultimate writing book for the starving artist who needs some humor and some spice.

Parisian Phoenix
PUBLISHING KINK

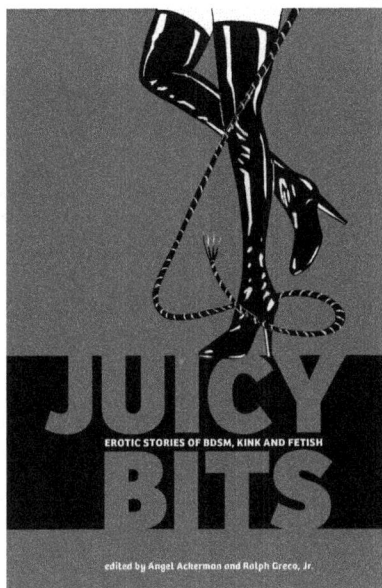

PARISIAN PHOENIX PUBLISHING KINK PRESENTS

JUICY BITS

Juicy Bits: Erotic Stories of BDSM, Kink & Fetish

From mild to wild—this book offers 25 erotic stories of BDSM, kink and fetish. Almost a dozen authors, from established voices in erotica to newcomers, fresh new characters to characters from existing fiction universes, these tales move the reader through a safe and consensual fantasies of exhibitionism, voyeurism, role play, sado-masochism, submission/dominance, impact play (and more) in labeled stories that allow the reader to explore the topics that intrigue them while skipping those that might be uncomfortable. Either way, the book provides a controlled, private opportunity to see what turns you on without taking your clothes off.

parisian phoenix
PUBLISHING KINK

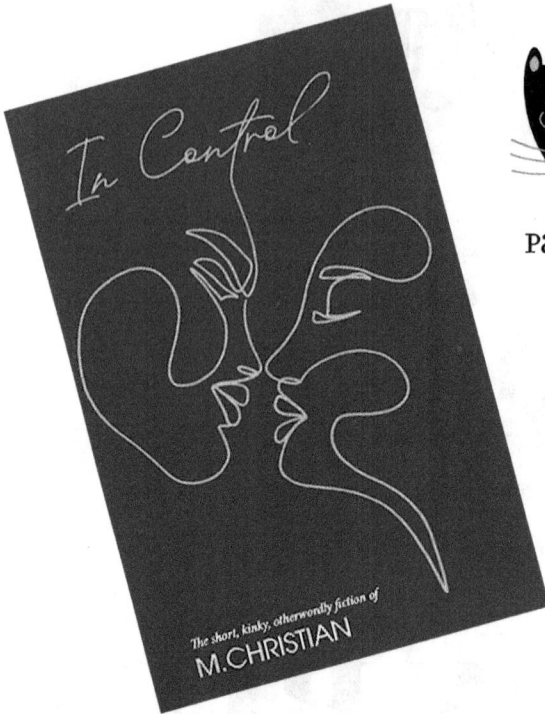

IN CONTROL

In this second edition release of a classic volume of short stories —
some more erotic than others, but all sensual and all with a
sense of otherwordly etherealness — M.Christian explores the
range of human emotion.

This book offers more than 15 stories delving into definitions
of domestic bliss, realization of fantasies, and everything from
self-control to finding freedom. Engaging with these stories should
titillate your intellect, offer fresh concepts of how people love,
and provide new insight into how people build relationships,
while warming your their body parts.

"M.Christian is a literary stylist of the highest caliber: smart,   funny, frightening,
sexy—there's nothing he can't write about ... and brilliantly."
—Tristan Taormino, author, speaker, sex educator, and activist

"M.Christian's fiction has a sexy logic all its own. He's inventive and he's irreverent.
His language can seduce, surprise, and body-slam you.
—Ceilia Tan, author, founder of Circlet Press

"Reading these tales is like climbing on for a sexual magic carpet ride through different
times and places, diverse bodies, and infinite possibilities."
—Carol Queen, author, sex educator